The Kids Book of
CANADI...
HISTORY

WRITTEN BY

Carlotta Hacker

ILLUSTRATED BY

John Mantha

KIDS CAN PRESS

Acknowledgements

I am most grateful to the following historians for their thoughtful advice and comments
during the preparation of this book: Dr. David M.L. Farr, Professor Emeritus, Department of History,
Carleton University; Professor John S. Milloy, Native Studies, Department of History, Trent University;
Professor Peter Neary, Department of History, University of Western Ontario; and Professor Sylvie Taschereau,
Département d'histoire, Université du Québec à Trois-Rivières. Their critiques were most valuable and of
great assistance, but they should not be held responsible for the contents of the book.
The final decision on what to include and how to present it was mine alone.

I also wish to thank Elizabeth Gonser, educator, for our discussions on how to give a balanced
view of complex historical events in a way that will be understood by a young audience.

For knowledgeable advice on the various details in the illustrations, I am grateful to Nora Trethewey,
historical re-enactor and costumer; Erika Romanowski of the London Museum of Archaeology;
and the staff of the Royal Canadian Military Institute.

Finally, I wish to say how much I appreciate the efforts of Kids Can editor Elizabeth MacLeod,
especially for her strong support throughout the project. — C.H.

First paperback edition 2009

Text © 2002 Carlotta Hacker
Illustrations © 2002 John Mantha

Kids Can Press acknowledges the financial support of the Ontario Arts Council,
the Canada Council for the Arts and the Government of Canada,
through the BPIDP, for our publishing activity.

Published in Canada by	Published in the U.S. by
Kids Can Press Ltd.	Kids Can Press Ltd.
29 Birch Avenue	2250 Military Road
Toronto, ON M4V 1E2	Tonawanda, NY 14150

www.kidscanpress.com

Edited by Elizabeth MacLeod
Designed by Julia Naimska
Printed and bound in China

The hardcover edition of this book is smyth sewn casebound.
The paperback edition of this book is limp sewn with a drawn-on cover.

CM 02 0 9 8 7 6 5 4
CM PA 09 0 9 8 7 6 5 4 3 2

Library and Archives Canada Cataloguing in Publication

Hacker, Carlotta, 1931–
The kids book of Canadian history / written by Carlotta Hacker ; illustrated by John Mantha.

Includes index.
ISBN 978-1-55074-868-0 (bound) ISBN 978-1-55453-328-2 (pbk.)

1. Canada — History — Juvenile literature. I. Mantha, John
II. Title.

FC172.H32 2002   j971   C2001-903738-4

Kids Can Press is a *lorus*™ Entertainment company

CONTENTS

CANADA'S FIRST PEOPLE

Canada's early history is an adventure story full of brave people and bold deeds. Some of the bravest were the very first people. They are thought to have come from Asia thousands of years ago, when a wide bridge of land linked Siberia and North America. They were following the animals they hunted.

These early people needed a lot of courage just to keep going. They must often have been tired and hungry. They would also have been cold — ice covered much of the world in summer as well as in winter. Over the centuries, as the earth warmed and the ice melted, they spread out across the continent.

First Nations

As time passed, the first people grouped themselves into nations — Algonquin, Beothuk, Cree and many others. Those in the Arctic called themselves Inuit. The different groups traded with one another and sometimes fought. All had strong spiritual beliefs, which they passed on through legends and stories. These beliefs were an important part of every Aboriginal culture.

Nations that lived in the same environment developed the same type of culture, based on the land and animals that provided their food and clothing. There were seven major cultural areas: Arctic, Subarctic, Eastern Woodlands (hunters), Eastern Woodlands (farmers), Plains, Plateau and Northwest Coast.

The seven main cultural areas of Canada's First People were:

- *Arctic*
- *Subarctic*
- *Northwest Coast*
- *Plains*
- *Plateau*
- *Eastern Woodlands (hunters)*
- *Eastern Woodlands (farmers)*

Nobody can say for sure when the early people came to North America. Some scientists think the very first groups arrived as much as 40 000 years ago. Many Aboriginal people do not agree with this theory. They believe their ancestors began here rather than coming from Asia.

Inuit of the Arctic

It took great skill just to stay alive in the Arctic, with its harsh climate and bitterly cold winters. Yet the Inuit developed a culture that included music, games, storytelling and other traditions. Much of this social activity took place during the long dark winters when many families camped together, living in snow houses (igloos). Seal-oil lamps kept the igloos snug and warm.

In summer, the Inuit built houses made of sod, or they camped in tents made of sealskin or caribou skin. Sometimes they gathered at favourite fishing spots, but for much of the year they were on the move, hunting in small family groups. Seals and caribou were the main animals hunted. They provided almost everything the Inuit needed, including food, clothing and a wide range of tools. Even their kayaks — slender hunting boats — were made mainly of sealskin.

Inuit means "the people." One person is an inuk.

Hunters of the Subarctic and Eastern Woodlands

The Subarctic stretches right across Canada, south of the Arctic. The people of this region were gatherers and hunters. They picked berries and hunted caribou and other animals. But animals and plants were scarce in this region, so most families had to keep moving to find enough to eat.

The hunters of the Eastern Woodlands lived in the forests that stretched from the Great Lakes to the Atlantic Ocean. Like the Subarctic people, they hunted in small bands and travelled by birchbark canoe or toboggan. But food was easier to find here, and some families lived in villages for part of the year.

Lacrosse was invented by the people of the Eastern Woodlands. It was called baggataway.

The Great Peace

Dekanahwideh was a famous peacemaker and lawgiver who is said to have lived in the Eastern Woodlands toward the end of the fifteenth century. To stop the nations from fighting one another, Dekanahwideh planted a huge white pine tree — the Tree of the Great Peace. Under it he buried weapons of the Seneca, Onondaga, Cayuga, Oneida and Mohawk nations. He then announced the Great Law of Peace, setting out how these nations should govern themselves as a group of allies.

The allies became known as the Iroquois Confederacy, or Five Nations — a very powerful group. Later, when the Tuscarora joined, they became the Six Nations. Today, many Iroquois still try to follow the law Dekanahwideh gave them.

they were highly respected. But they couldn't order people to obey them — they could only persuade. Each village held council meetings to decide village matters. There were also council meetings where the village chiefs met to make decisions for the whole nation. All decisions were made after long discussions, because everyone was allowed a say.

Farmers of the Eastern Woodlands

The farming people lived among the Great Lakes in what is now Ontario and New York state. Their chief crops were corn, beans and squash. Some also grew tobacco, which was used in spiritual and social ceremonies.

The people lived in large villages that were surrounded by palisades — fences of wooden stakes. Each village contained a number of longhouses made of bark laid over wooden frames. Several related families lived in each longhouse. Each family had its own living area but shared a cooking fire with another family. A row of fires ran down the centre of the longhouse, and raised sleeping platforms lined each side.

A senior woman was the head of the longhouse. Women had a lot of power because the farming nations traced family relationships through the mother, and children belonged to the mother's clan, not the father's. The senior women took part in all important decisions and chose the chiefs.

All the chiefs were men, and

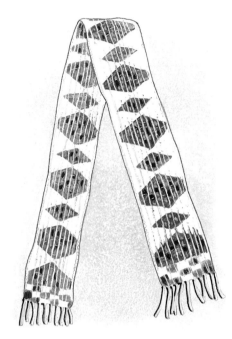

The people of the Eastern Woodlands kept a record of important events by weaving patterns on belts of coloured shells. These belts were called wampum.

Several families lived in each longhouse.

People of the Plains and Plateau

The Plains people lived on the prairies. They were hunters who followed the huge herds of buffalo that roamed the region. The buffalo provided almost everything these people needed. Their meat was the main food, and their thick hides were made into many things, including covers for tepees — cone-shaped tents. The bones were made into knives and other implements.

Buffalo hunts were often major events, involving hundreds of people who came together to hunt and hold spiritual ceremonies. The most important ceremony was the Sun Dance, which was celebrated each summer.

The Sun Dance was also celebrated by some of the Plateau people, who lived in the mountains west of the prairies. But the Plateau lifestyle was different. In winter, families lived in "pit houses." These were big holes dug in the ground and covered with branches and grass. The Plateau people netted salmon in the rivers and hunted deer and other mountain animals. In fact, they had more in common with the nations living west of them, on the coast, than they did with the Plains people.

Northwest Coast village.

Fishers of the Northwest Coast

The nations on the Pacific Coast lived in a mild climate and had plenty of food. In the lush rain forest, there were berries and edible roots as well as deer and other animals. But their main source of food was salmon. Millions of salmon swam up the rivers each year.

Because living was easy, the Coast people could develop a culture that was rich with art, music and grand ceremonies. They lived in villages of wooden houses made from the rain forest's cedar trees. Several families lived in each house, and each house had a leader.

Coast society was very structured, with people holding different ranks. There were slaves, commoners and chiefs, some chiefs ranking higher than others. As in other Aboriginal societies, chiefs were followed because they were respected. But here, the respect was based on the property a chief owned rather than on his bravery or wisdom.

Property included names, songs and crests as well as material objects. The crests were designs with special meanings. They were carved on tall totem poles. Like other property, crests were passed on to a relative when the owner died.

Potlatch

The potlatch was a ceremony of feasting, singing, dancing and acting. It was the most important event in Coast society and could take years to arrange. The chief giving the potlatch invited many people and gave them all presents.

The most valued presents were coppers — large sheets of copper hammered into the shape of a shield. If a chief wanted to be very impressive, he publicly destroyed his own coppers and other goods. The potlatch could leave him with very few possessions, but it brought him great power. Because of his generosity, all his guests owed him a favour, and he could call on them to do as he asked.

THE EUROPEANS ARRIVE

Like Aboriginal people, early Europeans travelled great distances, risking danger and death as they explored unknown territories. Why did they do it? Some had no choice. Wars or overcrowding drove them from home, and they needed somewhere new to live. Others explored out of curiosity — to find out what was there. Many hoped to find gold or other riches.

The Vikings

The Vikings were great sailors. They used winds and currents to take them across the Atlantic. Setting out from Scandinavia (today's Norway, Sweden and Denmark), they formed settlements in Iceland and Greenland in the ninth and tenth centuries.

The first European to see North America was probably a Viking named Bjarni, whose ship was blown off course on the way to Greenland. Bjarni sailed along the coast but didn't go ashore. About 15 years later, around A.D. 1000, Leif Ericsson decided to investigate the land Bjarni had seen. He landed in a country he named Helluland

Some Europeans went east as far as China searching for riches. They brought back jewels, silks, spices and other Asian goods, which were greatly valued in Europe. At first, most Europeans didn't explore west across the Atlantic. They thought there was nothing there except ocean — and probably huge sea monsters. But the Vikings knew better.

(probably Baffin Island), then sailed south, landing twice more — at Markland (possibly Labrador) and Vinland (probably Newfoundland).

Leif and his crew spent the winter in Vinland. When they returned to Greenland, their glowing reports caused others to go and settle there. But the settlement didn't last. The Aboriginal people didn't want these fierce invaders, and they drove the Vikings away.

The remains of a Viking settlement have been found at L'Anse aux Meadows, Newfoundland.

The Treasure Hunt Begins

By the fifteenth century, fishermen from Portugal and other European countries were sailing far into the Atlantic. Some may have fished in the waters off Newfoundland, but these good fishing grounds weren't widely known. It was John Cabot and his crew who spread news of them after his voyage of 1497.

Cabot was searching for treasure, not fish. He was trying to find a quick route to the riches of Asia. Like Christopher Columbus five years earlier, Cabot believed he could get to India or China by sailing west across the Atlantic. But he wanted to look farther north than Columbus had.

With the backing of some English businessmen, Cabot sailed from England in early May 1497. When he sighted land on June 24, he thought he'd reached China! In fact, he was in North America, probably on the coast of Newfoundland. To mark his arrival, Cabot planted a flag and claimed the region for England.

When Cabot returned to England and described the land he'd found, he told of seas teeming with fish. The sea was so full of cod, he said, that you could catch them just by lowering a basket into the water. This was exciting news. Fish were an important food item in fifteenth-

DID YOU KNOW

Explorers often captured people to take home along with other souvenirs. They did this to show that they really had been somewhere new and weren't making up stories. Usually, the captives caught European diseases and died.

PROFILE

JOHN CABOT

John Cabot (born Giovanni Caboto) was a trader in the state of Venice, which is now part of Italy. Since nobody in Venice would sponsor his voyage, he went to England for help. As a result, the first European claims to North America were made in the name of England. Cabot set out on a follow-up expedition in 1498 but was never heard of again.

century Europe. Soon, fishing ships from many nations were heading for the Grand Banks of Newfoundland. They continued to come, year after year, for centuries.

More Treasure Hunters

During the early 1500s, explorers as well as fishermen came to the east coast of North America. By then, Europeans had explored farther and knew that this land wasn't China or India. But they did expect to find great wealth. Farther south, the Spanish were filling their ships with silver, gold and sparkling jewels, which they'd taken from the people of Central and South America. It seemed logical to expect similar treasure in the north.

Cabot's ship, the **Matthew,** *took seven weeks to cross the Atlantic.*

Jacques Cartier Arrives

In 1534, the king of France sent Jacques Cartier across the Atlantic with two ships. He hoped Cartier would find gold or a sea route to Asia. Cartier reached Newfoundland in May, found his way through the Strait of Belle Isle and explored the Gulf of St. Lawrence. On July 24, he set up a large cross on the Gaspé Peninsula as a sign that he was claiming this country for France.

At Gaspé, Cartier traded with a group of Iroquois who had come there to fish, and he made friends with the chief, Donnacona. When Cartier left for France, he tricked two of Donnacona's sons into coming with him.

Cartier's Second Voyage

Cartier came back the next year, bringing Donnacona's sons with him. The young men showed him the way into the St. Lawrence River and took him to their village of Stadacona, where Quebec City stands today. As Cartier sailed up this great river, he was very excited — he thought he'd found a waterway to the Pacific. But when he later followed the St. Lawrence farther inland, his way was blocked by rapids.

Cartier and his men spent the winter at Stadacona. They had never known such cold. Their European clothes gave them little protection from the bitter wind and driving snow. Worse, many of the men died of scurvy, a disease caused by lack of vitamin C. Only when they learned from the Iroquois how to make a drink from cedar bark and leaves did they stop getting sick.

By then, the Iroquois and French were no longer good friends. Each group mistrusted the other. Before sailing home in the spring of 1536, Cartier kidnapped Donnacona and a few other Iroquois. Although these captives were treated well in France, most of them got sick and died.

Quick Facts
Some Explorers of North America

Year	Explorer	Sailing for
1497	John Cabot arrives at Newfoundland.	England
1500, 1501	Gaspar Corte-Real scouts the coast of Labrador and Newfoundland.	Portugal
1524	Giovanni da Verrazzano explores the east coast from Florida to Newfoundland.	France
1534, 1535–36, and 1541–42	Jacques Cartier explores the Gulf of St. Lawrence and enters the St. Lawrence River.	France

The Third Voyage

Cartier's return without his captives in 1541 increased the Iroquois' mistrust of the French. Before long, the two groups were fighting and killing one another. The Iroquois also attacked a group of French settlers who came to start a colony. Yet when Cartier set sail for France in 1542, he felt triumphant. His ships were full of rocks that glinted with shining particles — gold and diamonds, Cartier was sure.

But the rocks proved to be worthless. The attempt at settlement failed, too. The French were so discouraged that 60 years passed before they again showed much interest in Canada.

Gilbert claiming Newfoundland.

Newfoundland: Britain's First Colony

Like Cartier, the English explorer Sir Humphrey Gilbert hoped to find a waterway to the Pacific. He also hoped to start a settlement in North America. On a voyage in 1583, he called in at Newfoundland and claimed it for England. Although 36 fishing boats from various nations were already in the harbour, none dared oppose Gilbert, who had with him a fleet of warships.

Gilbert then sailed away, was lost in a storm and drowned. But because of his action, Newfoundland became a British colony. There were now two nations that had made strong claims to this region — France and England.

Canada got its name because of a mistake. The Huron–Iroquois word for "village" is *kanata*. When Donnacona's sons pointed in the direction of their village, Cartier thought they were telling him the name of the country.

The Northwest Passage

When no sea route could be found through North America, explorers looked for it farther north. One of the first to seek this Northwest Passage was Sir Martin Frobisher, who made three voyages to the Arctic — in 1576, 1577 and 1578. He didn't find the passage, but he thought he'd found gold. On his third voyage, he took 15 ships and brought back hundreds of tons of rock. But the rocks didn't contain even one speck of gold.

In 1610, another Arctic explorer, Henry Hudson, sailed into the bay that was later named after him. His crew mutinied and forced him into a small boat, along with his son and some sick sailors. Hudson was never seen again. But the bay he had found was to become very important.

MEETING OF CULTURES

By 1600, Europeans had discovered that North America did, after all, have great riches — a vast amount of furs. Fishermen who came to the coast found they could buy beautiful furs from Aboriginal people by offering kettles, knives and other metal goods. Both groups were parting with something very ordinary in return for something they valued greatly.

The most valuable furs were beaver pelts because the beaver's soft under-fur was used to make high-quality felt, and felt hats were the latest fashion in Europe. Eager to obtain the pelts, French merchants sent traders across the Atlantic each summer. Soon the French and Aboriginal people were trading regularly.

Port-Royal

In 1605, a group of French fur traders built Port-Royal, a small cluster of wooden buildings in what is now Nova Scotia. They had arrived the previous year and spent a terrible winter on the other side of the Bay of Fundy (on St. Croix Island at the mouth of the St. Croix River). Almost half the group had died of hunger or scurvy. Now the survivors were hoping to do better in a more protected place.

They did do better. They planted vegetables and wheat and made friends with the local Mi'kmaq people, who brought them meat as well as furs. Among the French group was a young map maker and explorer named Samuel de Champlain. He kept the group happy by inventing the Order of Good Cheer — a sort of social club that put on entertainments and feasts.

In 1608, he was sent to the St. Lawrence River to start a fur-trading post there. As leader, Champlain was to govern the settlement as well as run the fur trade.

◆ PROFILE ◆

SAMUEL DE CHAMPLAIN

Samuel de Champlain was a cheerful man who got on well with people, including Aboriginal people. He became an ally of the Huron, who acted as "middlemen" in the fur trade — they traded for furs with hunters farther north, then sold these furs to the French.

Champlain explored and mapped much of the region, going inland as far as Georgian Bay. Meanwhile, he encouraged the few settlers to take up farming and develop a strong community. His whole life was devoted to building the colony known as New France.

The Fur-Trade Monopoly

The king of France wanted a colony in North America to bring him wealth and glory, but he couldn't afford to set one up. So he gave a group of traders a monopoly. This meant they were the only people allowed to trade in furs. In return, they had to bring out settlers and priests. They also had to appoint a governor, who would rule on behalf of the king. Different trading groups held the monopoly at different times. The largest was the Company of One Hundred Associates, formed in 1627.

Jeanne Mance came to Montreal with Maisonneuve's group. She nursed the sick and wounded and started Montreal's first hospital, the Hôtel-Dieu.

Early Days at Quebec

Champlain called his new trading post Quebec, after a local word meaning "where the river narrows." He traded with Algonquin and Montagnais people, who soon asked him to help fight their enemy, the Iroquois. Champlain felt bound to do so in order to keep their friendship.

In the first battle, Champlain shot two Iroquois chiefs dead and wounded another. The Iroquois fled in terror. They had never seen a gun before. But they later obtained guns by trading with the Dutch, who had settlements farther south. Before long, the Iroquois were terrorizing the French.

The French were also threatened by a long-standing enemy — the English. The two nations were often at war, and in 1629 an English force sailed up the St. Lawrence and captured Quebec. But the French got it back when a peace treaty was signed in 1632.

The Struggle for Survival

Very few settlers arrived during the early years. The fur-trading merchants weren't eager to bring people to New France. It cost a lot of money and didn't help the fur trade. But little by little, the colony grew.

In 1642, a nobleman, the Sieur de Maisonneuve, brought a group of missionaries to start a settlement on the island of Montreal. The people at Quebec said he was crazy — the

island was controlled by the Iroquois. During the next few years, the Iroquois launched attack after attack on Maisonneuve's settlement of Ville-Marie. But it held out and grew to be the town of Montreal.

Hurons and Black Robes

Like Maisonneuve's group, a number of priests and nuns had come to New France to teach Christianity to Aboriginal people. Jesuit priests travelled far into Huron territory near Georgian Bay to set up missions in the villages. Some Huron were converted, but many disliked being told that their religion was evil. Also, they blamed the black-robed priests for the diseases that were killing so many of them.

Measles, smallpox and other common European diseases were new to North America, and Aboriginal people had no resistance against them. The Huron were especially hard hit because of their close contact with the French. As the Huron became weaker, the Iroquois became more powerful.

Some Jesuit priests taught Christianity in Huron villages.

NEW FRANCE

The situation was grim. The Iroquois had grown so strong that the French were trapped inside their settlements. When they went into the fields to harvest their crops, they risked being killed.

Aboriginal people were dying in even greater numbers. The fur trade had increased the warfare among them because they all wanted the beaver pelts that bought European goods. The Iroquois could get goods from the Dutch and English farther south, but they needed high-quality pelts. The best were in the north, so they ambushed the Huron canoes that were taking furs to the French. The attacks became fiercer and more terrible each year.

A Time of Crisis

The main fur-trade route from the beaver-rich country of the Canadian Shield was down the Ottawa River to Montreal and Quebec, where the furs were shipped to France. As the Iroquois attacks on the Huron canoe fleets increased, fewer and fewer got through. This was a disaster for the French as well as the Huron. The French needed the income from the furs in order to keep the colony going.

Worse was to follow. In 1648 and 1649, the Iroquois swept through Huron country, setting fire to the villages and scattering the inhabitants. Many were killed, including some of the Jesuit priests. By the late 1650s, the Iroquois had defeated all their Aboriginal rivals. They then turned their full force on the French, determined to drive them from the continent.

"THEY COME LIKE FOXES THROUGH THE WOODS. THEY ATTACK LIKE LIONS. THEY TAKE FLIGHT LIKE BIRDS, DISAPPEARING BEFORE THEY HAVE REALLY APPEARED."

Jérôme Lalemant, Jesuit missionary, describing the Iroquois style of fighting

15

Rescued

To save his colony, King Louis XIV cancelled the fur-trade company's monopoly in 1663 and made New France a royal colony run by him. He sent out soldiers to help the settlers fight the Iroquois, and a peace treaty was signed in 1667. War broke out again in 1680, but another peace was made in 1701.

There were fewer than 3000 people in New France in 1663, but more were willing to come once the warfare ended. Since most of the population was male, the king sent hundreds of women to New France to marry the men. These women were called *filles du roi* (daughters of the king). Many were orphans. Others were poor, unmarried women who saw the chance of a better life overseas. On arrival, they stayed with nuns, who helped choose their husbands.

How the People Lived

The king gave large blocks of land to men called *seigneurs*, who kept some for themselves and leased the rest to farmers called *habitants*. Most blocks of land were along rivers, because rivers were the "roads" of New France.

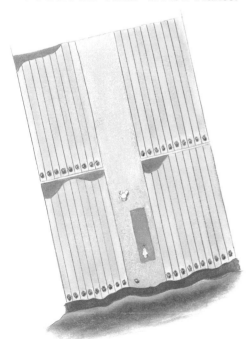

Plan of a seigneury.

Although habitants didn't own their land, they could pass it on to their children — generally to their sons. Since each son needed access to the river, the land was divided into strips rather than squares. The strips got thinner as the land was passed down.

Most habitants' houses were wooden, and many had only one room. But there was always a huge stone fireplace, used for cooking as well as heating. The houses had no running water, and the only form of indoor toilet was a bucket or a pot under the bed. As well as working on the farm, habitants made most of their furniture and clothes. Most children didn't go to school but were taught religion by the local priest.

Quick Facts
Duties of Seigneurs and Habitants

A seigneur had to	A habitant had to
• lease land to habitants	• build a house and start a farm
• build a house and mill	• pay the seigneur a small rent
• pay part of the cost of building a church	• give some of his crops to the seigneur
• help build bridges and roads	• work on the seigneur's land for a few days each year

Life in the Towns

New France had three towns — Quebec, Montreal and Trois-Rivières. They were far wealthier than the countryside. Fur-trading merchants lived in solid stone houses. Other stone buildings housed priests and nuns of the Catholic Church, who ran schools and hospitals as well as giving religious services.

Quebec was the most important town, home of the governor and other powerful people. It was also the main port and was especially busy during the summer, when ships arrived from France. But Montreal was gaining in importance because of the fur trade. It was from Montreal that French explorers set out to spread the fur trade — and French territory — far across the continent.

Government under the King

As a royal colony, New France was ruled by a governor, intendant and bishop, all of whom reported to the king through his chief minister in France. The governor was head of the military as well as the government. The intendant dealt with the daily business of the colony, and the bishop was in charge of religion. All three were members of the Sovereign Council, which included other appointed men. The Council made the laws and was also the colony's highest law court.

Famous members of the Sovereign Council were Jean Talon (intendant, 1665–68 and 1669–72), the Comte de Frontenac (governor, 1672–82 and 1689–98) and François de Laval (bishop, 1674–88).

Jean Talon

Comte de Frontenac

François de Laval

TRADERS & EXPLORERS

In the late 1600s and the 1700s, explorers spread farther and farther across the continent. Some of these adventurers were missionaries, but most were fur traders. They were looking for places that still had plenty of beaver or other animals. They also wanted to find more Aboriginal nations to trade with.

New France got most of its money from the fur trade, so it was against the law for people to trade privately and keep all the profits for themselves. But after the Iroquois stopped attacking the French, young Frenchmen began to slip away to the woods to trap or trade for beaver on their own. This was far more fun than working on the family farm. These illegal traders were called *coureurs des bois* (runners of the woods).

Radisson and Des Groseilliers

Pierre-Esprit Radisson was a coureur des bois. He had been captured by the Iroquois as a child and adopted by a Mohawk family, so he knew how to survive in the forests. Because of these skills, he dared to leave the French settlements even at the height of the Iroquois wars.

In 1659–60, Radisson and his brother-in-law, Médard Chouart Des Groseilliers, travelled to the west of Lake Superior, where they traded for furs. They collected so many beaver pelts that they needed 300 Aboriginal people to paddle their fleet of canoes home to New France.

This was at a time when the fur trade was at a standstill because of the Iroquois raids. But the Iroquois weren't guarding the river at that moment, having just fought a week-long battle. The French settlers couldn't believe their eyes when they saw canoe after canoe sweeping down the St. Lawrence. New France was saved — at least for a while. But the governor wasn't pleased. He was furious that the two men had gone trading without his permission.

North to Hudson Bay

The governor fined Radisson and Des Groseilliers and made them pay an extra large tax on their furs. And neither he nor anyone in France would sponsor a further expedition — even though the two had heard there were lots of beaver in the north, near Hudson Bay.

Radisson and Des Groseilliers eventually found backing in England. In 1668, a group of British businessmen sent them to Hudson Bay with two ships. Only one ship, the *Nonsuch* (right), got as far as the bay, but the magnificent furs it brought back impressed everyone, including the British king, Charles II.

In 1670, the king granted a charter to this "company of adventurers," giving them control of all the land drained by rivers flowing into Hudson Bay. He named the region Rupert's Land, after his cousin, who was first governor of what became known as the Hudson's Bay Company.

DID YOU KNOW

None of the explorers could have succeeded without the help of Aboriginal people, who guided and fed them. They travelled the Aboriginal way — by canoe, snowshoes and toboggan — and learned many other Aboriginal skills.

The Battle of the Long Sault, 1660

At the Long Sault rapids near Montreal, Adam Dollard Des Ormeaux and most of his men died fighting a week-long battle against hundreds of Iroquois.

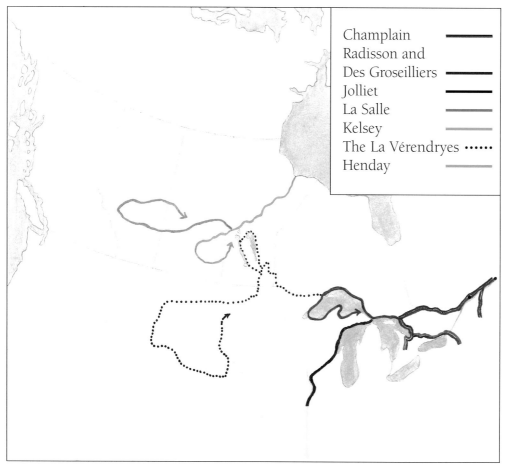

Legend:
- Champlain
- Radisson and Des Groseilliers
- Jolliet
- La Salle
- Kelsey
- The La Vérendryes
- Henday

French Explorations

Like Jacques Cartier, some French explorers still hoped to find a waterway to the Pacific Ocean. In 1673, the trader-explorer Louis Jolliet set out to find "the great river they call the Mississippi" and travel along it until he reached the Pacific. Guided by Aboriginal people, he and his small group did find the Mississippi,

but turned back when they realized it was taking them south, not west.

Nine years later, the fiery René-Robert Cavelier de La Salle set out to find where the Mississippi went. After following it to its mouth in the Gulf of Mexico, he claimed the whole region for France. He named it Louisiana, after the king.

Much of the west became French territory because of the explorations of Pierre Gaultier de La Vérendrye (left) and his sons. In the 1730s and 1740s, they built a string of trading posts from Lake Superior all the way to the Saskatchewan River.

English Explorations

The English didn't at first go inland. Instead, they asked hunters to bring furs to the British trading forts on Hudson Bay. Hoping to get distant hunters to come to the forts, the Hudson's Bay Company (HBC) sent Henry Kelsey on a long journey southwest in 1690 to meet with the Aboriginal people there. He

Price of Trade Goods

The beaver on the nickel is a reminder that beaver pelts were once used as money. Blankets, fish hooks and all other trade goods were priced in pelts. In 1720, four knives cost one beaver pelt. A gun cost 14 pelts.

was the first European to see the Canadian prairies and the first to see buffalo and grizzly bears.

In 1754, another HBC employee, Anthony Henday (below), went as far as present-day Alberta, where he tried to persuade the Blackfoot people to bring their furs to Hudson Bay. But the Blackfoot weren't interested. They were already getting goods from Aboriginal "middlemen," who traded with the French as well as the English.

The rivalry between French and English traders often led to fighting. They captured each other's forts and sank each other's ships. They were especially aggressive whenever France and England were at war, because war in Europe meant war in North America, too.

WAR!

England and France were almost constantly at war, and by the early 1700s they were locked in a struggle for North America. Both nations claimed Rupert's Land, Newfoundland and Acadia (today's Maritimes). Farther south, down the Atlantic coast, were England's 13 American colonies. Behind them was New France, which stretched from the Gulf of St. Lawrence to the Gulf of Mexico.

The big battles were fought mostly by British and French troops, but the settlers played an important part. The *Canadiens* (as French settlers were now called) had learned to fight the Iroquois way, and they ambushed the English in the forests. But the English won many of the larger battles.

Two Powerful Rivals

The French and English fought at sea as well as on land. French ships raided Newfoundland's settlements, and British ships attacked Acadia. In 1690, a fleet from Boston sailed up the St. Lawrence and demanded the surrender of Quebec. But Governor Frontenac stood firm, threatening to fire on the fleet.

Port-Royal changed hands several times, and in 1713 the French lost it permanently. By the Treaty of Utrecht, which ended an 11-year war, the British gained Port-Royal along with much of Acadia — which they called Nova Scotia.

"MY ONLY REPLY WILL COME FROM THE MOUTHS OF MY CANNONS AND MUSKETS."

Frontenac, 1690

Quick Facts
Treaty of Utrecht, 1713

• *Britain kept Nova Scotia (which included part of today's New Brunswick).*

• *France kept the rest of Acadia (including today's Prince Edward Island and Cape Breton Island).*

• *France gave up its claims to Rupert's Land and Newfoundland.*

• *French fishermen could still land and dry their fish on Newfoundland's French Shore (on part of the northeast and west coasts).*

The Acadians

The French settlers in Nova Scotia didn't expect things to change much now that they were in a British colony. In the past, they had just gone on farming whether they were under French or English rule.

The Acadians were independent people who lived off what they grew on their farms. The best farms were on the shores of the Bay of Fundy, where the Acadians had drained the salt marshes. A system of dykes kept the sea out, protecting the land from the high tides. During low tide, the farmers opened gates in the dykes to let rainwater and melted snow flow out. This gradually washed the salt out of the marshes and created rich farmland.

PIERRE LE MOYNE D'IBERVILLE

Pierre Le Moyne d'Iberville was New France's great naval hero. A fearless adventurer, he terrorized the English, sinking their ships and destroying their settlements. His most famous victory was in Hudson Bay, where his ship *Pélican* defeated three British warships in 1697.

Louisbourg

Although Nova Scotia was a British colony, almost everyone there was Acadian or Aboriginal. So, in 1749, Governor Edward Cornwallis arrived with 2500 English-speaking settlers. They built the town of Halifax. More settlers came later, but they were still outnumbered by the Acadians, and this worried the British.

The French military had built the fortress of Louisbourg on Île Royale (Cape Breton Island) and clearly hoped to take back Nova Scotia. What if the Acadians sided with them? The British wanted the Acadians to take an oath of loyalty, but the Acadians refused — it could mean they would have to fight fellow Frenchmen.

Louisbourg became France's main military base and port on the Atlantic coast.

The End of New France

The battle that decided the fate of North America lasted barely 15 minutes. It took place at Quebec in 1759. For weeks, General James Wolfe had been trying to take Quebec, but the walled city was strongly defended by the Marquis de Montcalm's forces.

Wolfe's officers finally suggested a surprise attack. On the night of September 12, the British crept up the cliffs to the Plains of Abraham. Next morning, the French had a horrible shock — they saw thousands of British soldiers lined up on the plains. Most of the French troops defending Quebec were Canadiens, who could fight well in the woods but weren't trained for formal battles. As they charged toward the British, they were mown down by musket fire. Wolfe and Montcalm both died as a result of the battle.

The French surrendered the next year, after the British captured Montreal. By the Treaty of Paris, which formally ended the Seven Years' War in 1763, France lost all its North American possessions except St-Pierre and Miquelon — two small islands off the south coast of Newfoundland. They still belong to France today.

The Deportations

When fighting started again, leading to the Seven Years' War, Lieutenant-Governor Charles Lawrence decided to *make* the Acadians swear the oath. As usual, they refused. So in 1755 he had them driven off the land — rich farming land, which English settlers wanted. British soldiers rounded up the Acadians, burned their homes and forced them into ships, which took them south to the American colonies or across the Atlantic to France or England.

Many families were separated. Some people were killed, and others died at sea. A few escaped, but the deportations continued year after year until almost all the Acadians were removed from the region.

Thousands of Acadians were forced to leave their homes in 1755. During the deportations, many families became separated and never saw their relatives again.

General James Wolfe

Marquis de Montcalm

NEWCOMERS IN THE EAST

"What will happen to us now?" Canadiens asked one another when New France fell to the British. They had seen what had happened to the Acadians. But the situation on the St. Lawrence was different. The population of Acadia had been about 13 000. Here it was about 65 000, plus about 5000 French soldiers who were staying on as settlers. The British couldn't deport so many people.

Instead, they aimed to assimilate the Canadiens — to make them part of a larger English-speaking community so that the French language and culture would eventually die out. The British thought that thousands of settlers from the American colonies would soon move north to the Province of Quebec, as the new British colony was called. So they organized Quebec like other British colonies.

The Royal Proclamation of 1763

The Royal Proclamation of 1763 has been called "The Indian Bill of Rights." As well as establishing the Province of Quebec, it laid down the ground rules for all future negotiations over Aboriginal land. It set aside a large area as the Aboriginal people's "hunting grounds" and said that the land could not be taken from them without their agreement. Nor could it be bought by settlers.

Only the government could buy land from the First Nations. Before the sale took place, both sides had to sign a treaty agreeing to the terms. The proclamation therefore recognized that Aboriginal people owned the land on which they lived.

The British Take Over
The Royal Proclamation of 1763, which set up the colony, said that it would have English laws and, eventually, an elected Legislative Assembly (see page 27). This made Canadiens very unhappy.

By English law, only Protestants could take part in government, be a judge or sit on a jury. Since Canadiens were Catholics, they would have no say in running the colony. They were also losing control of business — British traders had taken over much of the fur trade in Montreal.

The Quebec Act

To make things better for Canadiens so that they wouldn't rebel, the British passed the Quebec Act of 1774. The Act allowed Catholics in Quebec to take part in government. As well, it gave back many other things Canadiens wanted, including French law. Only criminal cases would be tried by British law.

The Act also made the colony much larger. Quebec now included the land surrounding the Great Lakes and spread southwest to the Mississippi and Ohio rivers. However, settlers couldn't occupy much of this land because it was the Aboriginal people's "hunting grounds." It was known as Indian Territory.

The American Revolution

The Quebec Act angered the people of the American colonies — the Thirteen Colonies on the eastern seaboard. Like the Royal Proclamation, it aimed to stop the colonies from spreading west into Indian Territory. Britain wanted to keep this area for Aboriginal people so that they could live their own lives — and trap furs for British traders in Montreal. But the

PROFILE

JOSEPH BRANT

The Mohawk chief Joseph Brant fought on the British side and persuaded other Mohawks to join him. After the revolution, the Indian Territory became part of the United States, so Brant moved his people to a large stretch of land they were granted along the Grand River (near today's Brantford, Ontario).

Thirteen Colonies needed more land. Settlers had already ignored the law by moving into the Ohio valley.

The American colonies were tired of taking orders from Britain. They were wealthy now and able to support themselves. They especially hated the high taxes Britain made them pay. The Quebec Act was one more thing that made them furious, one of the many things that led to the American Revolution.

The revolution started in 1775. That same year, the Americans captured Montreal and attacked Quebec City, but they were driven back in 1776. They had expected the French population to rebel, too, but the Canadiens didn't do so. The Quebec Act had solved their main problems, and their clergy advised against joining the Americans, who were strongly anti-Catholic.

Newfoundland and Nova Scotia also stayed loyal to Britain. So did thousands of people in the Thirteen Colonies. These Loyalists were helped by many Aboriginal people who wanted to stop American settlers from taking their land. As well, there were Black Loyalists — Britain had promised to free any slaves who escaped from their American owners to join the fighting.

DID YOU KNOW

Many of the Loyalists who settled in Nova Scotia brought their slaves with them. About 3500 Black Loyalists also arrived. Black and white Loyalists had both been promised grants of land and three years' worth of supplies. But most Black families got only three months' supplies and no land — or just a tiny plot. To survive, they had to work for the whites.

Quick Facts

When the colonies of British North America were formed

When formed	Colony
1713	Newfoundland (first claimed in 1583)
1713	Nova Scotia
1763	Province of Quebec
1769	Prince Edward Island (formerly part of Nova Scotia)
1784	New Brunswick (formerly part of Nova Scotia)
1791	Lower Canada (formerly part of Province of Quebec)
1791	Upper Canada (formerly part of Province of Quebec)

The Loyalists

The Americans sometimes punished Loyalists by painting them with boiling black tar and then covering them with feathers. Many Loyalists lived in fear of being "tarred and feathered." So while some fought in the war, others took their families to the safety of British territory.

When the Americans won and a peace treaty was signed in 1783, thousands more Loyalists left. Many went to Britain, but well over 40 000 fled north to the colonies of British North America. These colonies now included Prince Edward Island, where some Scots had settled after the Acadians were deported.

New Beginnings

So many Loyalists went to Nova Scotia that the British made part of it a separate colony called New Brunswick. They also encouraged Loyalists to take up land in the unsettled part of Quebec, west of the French-speaking communities. The government bought this land by making treaties with the Aboriginal people.

The western part of Quebec (today's Ontario) was a gloomy forest of huge trees. The Loyalists who settled there first had to chop down enough trees to make a clearing. Only then could they build a log house and plant some crops (below).

Upper Canada

Because the Loyalists were from British colonies, they had different traditions from the seigneurs and habitants in the St. Lawrence valley. So, in 1791, Quebec was divided into two colonies — Lower Canada, where most Canadiens lived, and Upper Canada for the Loyalists. The dividing line was the Ottawa River.

The first lieutenant-governor of Upper Canada was John Graves Simcoe. He had two highways cut through the forest (above) so that soldiers and settlers could move easily. To get more settlers, he advertised in the United States, offering land very cheaply. Other families came from Britain, either on their own or as part of an organized group. Huge blocks of land were given to favoured Loyalists or others, on condition that they fill their land with settlers. With so much effort put into settling Upper Canada, the population more than doubled in the next ten years.

The Constitutional Act of 1791

The Constitutional Act of 1791, which created Upper and Lower Canada, gave each colony "representative government." Under this system, settlers elected members to a Legislative Assembly, which could make laws and raise taxes. But the laws weren't passed unless the governor and his two councils approved. The Maritime colonies already had representative government. Nova Scotia had got it in 1758, Prince Edward Island in 1773 and New Brunswick in 1784. Newfoundland didn't get it until 1832.

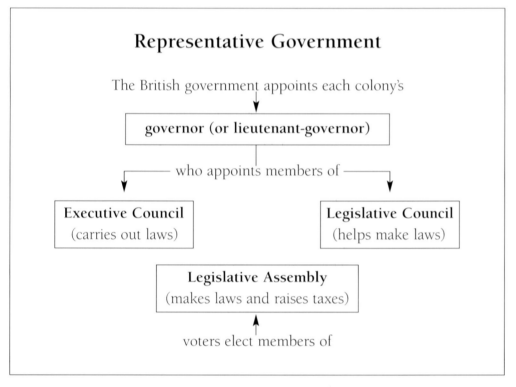

Representative Government

The British government appoints each colony's

governor (or lieutenant-governor)

who appoints members of

Executive Council
(carries out laws)

Legislative Council
(helps make laws)

Legislative Assembly
(makes laws and raises taxes)

voters elect members of

Fishing Admirals and Livyers

Each year, the captain of the first English ship to arrive in a Newfoundland harbour became the "fishing admiral" for that season. His job was to keep order and make sure that no one stayed behind in the fall. The fishing merchants didn't want a population of settlers, who would be rivals in the fishery. Early attempts at settlement had seldom lasted long, and the merchants wanted it to stay that way.

In spite of this, and in spite of raids by enemy ships, more and more people were living year-round in Newfoundland. These "livyers," as they were called, often fought the Beothuk, the Aboriginal people, and sometimes even hunted them. Each year, as the number of settlers increased, the number of Beothuk grew less until there were none left.

The English preserved fish by drying it in the sun at "fishing stations" along the Newfoundland coast.

Pirates and Fishermen

Far to the east, in Newfoundland, the population grew more slowly. The island had long been a dangerous place to live. Its coves and inlets provided a perfect hiding place for pirates, who attacked coastal settlements and raided passing ships. Many pirates had once been fishermen. The government allowed them to attack enemy ships in wartime, and they went on raiding in peacetime. But fishing was still the main business. Hundreds of ships crossed the Atlantic each year to catch cod in the seas around Newfoundland.

NEWCOMERS IN THE WEST

The Nootka people were terrified. Something huge and strange was coming in from the sea. Was it their god Qua-utz coming to punish them? Many Nootka fled to the mountains. Others bravely paddled out in their dugout canoes to meet the strange object.

It was a Spanish sailing ship, captained by Juan Pérez — a human, as the Nootka soon realized. Pérez was the first European to see Vancouver Island. He had on board a large wooden cross, which he intended to erect while claiming the land for Spain. But a strong wind suddenly came up, and he couldn't get ashore. Four years later, the English had better luck.

Europeans on the Coast

In 1778, Captain James Cook and his men spent a month at Nootka Sound on Vancouver Island. They were the first Europeans to land in what is now British Columbia. Within a few years, more English arrived, as well as the Spanish and Americans. All were eager to obtain the local sea-otter skins.

Much of this trade was handled by the Nootka chief Maquinna, a skilful diplomat. Maquinna played on the rivalry between the visiting traders to prevent them from taking advantage of him. But of course he couldn't know that both Britain and Spain were claiming the whole region as their own. After England's George Vancouver mapped the coast north to Alaska in 1792–94, Britain had the stronger claim.

Cook was welcomed by the Nootka (who are also called Nuu-chah-nulth).

Overland to the Pacific

Britain's claim was strengthened when fur traders from the east made their way overland to the Pacific coast. The Montreal fur trade was now run by British merchants, though most of their boatmen — the *voyageurs* — were French or Aboriginal. These groups spread the fur trade far across the continent.

Alexander Mackenzie

In 1778, Peter Pond was the first trader to get to the fur-rich Athabasca country south of Great Slave Lake. Pond's explorations spurred Alexander Mackenzie to follow the river that now bears his name, hoping it would take him to the Pacific Ocean. Instead, it took him to the Arctic Ocean. So Mackenzie and his voyageurs tried again, and in 1793 they reached the Pacific, but not by an easy river route. They had to hike much of the way.

DAVID THOMPSON

Fur trader David Thompson was one of the world's great geographers. He explored and mapped much of northwestern North America, and in 1811 traced the Columbia River its full length. But he wasn't famous in his lifetime. He lived in poverty during his last years — and gradually went blind.

Rival Traders

The traders were trying to find the source of the Columbia River so that they could take goods to the Pacific by boat instead of carrying them. Simon Fraser thought he was on the Columbia when in 1808 he set off down the river named after him. But the river was no good as a trade route because of its fierce rapids.

Like Pond and Mackenzie, Fraser was a member of the North West Company (NWC), a group of Montreal traders. The traders had banded together to compete with the Hudson's Bay Company (HBC), which no longer did business only from Hudson Bay. In 1774, the HBC had sent Samuel Hearne to build Cumberland House, west of Lake Winnipeg. The HBC had since built more inland trading forts (below) — usually right next to rival trading posts.

The Red River Settlement

The rivalry between the trading companies grew very bitter when the HBC started a settlement on the prairies at Red River. It was organized by a Scottish aristocrat, Lord Selkirk, who wanted to give poor British families a better life.

The Nor'westers — the NWC men — were strongly against the project because the land given to the settlement spread over a vast area, blocking their trade routes. Also, they feared that the herds of buffalo would move away if farmers moved in. The fur trade in the prairies was based on the buffalo.

The first settlers arrived at Red River in 1812. In the next few years, their crops failed, their sheep died and they almost starved. Their only friends were a few Aboriginal people. The settlers' leader, Miles Macdonell, didn't get on well with the HBC traders, and he was hated by the Nor'westers and their Métis allies.

The Métis

The Métis (meaning "mixed") were of both European and Aboriginal origin. Since the early days, traders had formed relationships with Aboriginal women and in many cases had married them. The women played an important role in the fur trade, travelling with the men and often translating or negotiating for them.

The Métis hunted buffalo, whose skins they traded, and they made the pemmican that traders ate on long journeys. Macdonell wanted pemmican for his settlers in case they ran out of food, so he announced that none was to be taken out of the settlement. This so angered the Nor'westers and Métis that they attacked the settlers' homes and burned their crops, hoping to drive them away.

In the fighting that followed, people on both sides were killed. But peace was eventually restored, and in 1821 the NWC became part of the HBC. The HBC now had charge of all British territory in the North and West, including the Red River Settlement. As the years passed, many fur traders retired to the settlement, and it became the centre of Métis life.

Pemmican

Pemmican was made from dried buffalo meat, which was pounded and then boiled together with fat and berries. When the mixture cooled, it hardened and could be cut into chunks. It was a basic food of the Aboriginal hunters of the prairies because it would keep for a long time and was easy to carry.

THE WAR OF 1812

While the fur traders were battling on the prairies, the British North American colonies farther east were fighting a full-scale war against the United States. The war was sparked by British actions at sea. Britain was in the midst of yet another war against France, and the Royal Navy had set up a blockade to prevent ships from taking supplies to France. This hurt American trade.

Worse still, the British stopped and searched ships at sea, looking for deserters from the Royal Navy. When two captured deserters turned out to be American, people in the United States were furious. Although the two men were released, the incident gave the United States an excuse to go to war with Britain. And war with Britain meant war with its North American colonies.

War Hawks

Many Americans wanted the war. They wanted to stop Montreal fur traders from selling guns to the Aboriginal people of the Ohio valley — the region known as Indian Territory. Now that this region was part of the United States, more and more settlers were moving in, and the Aboriginal people were fighting back. Americans suspected the British of helping the Shawnee leader Tecumseh. He was trying to form an alliance of First Nations that would be strong enough to stop settlers from moving any farther west.

But the Americans were determined to move west. Their population was growing, and they needed more land. Many also wanted to move north. They thought the whole continent should belong to the United States. So in 1812 an army crossed the Detroit River and invaded Upper Canada.

"THE ACQUISITION OF CANADA … WILL BE A MERE MATTER OF MARCHING."

Thomas Jefferson, former U.S. president

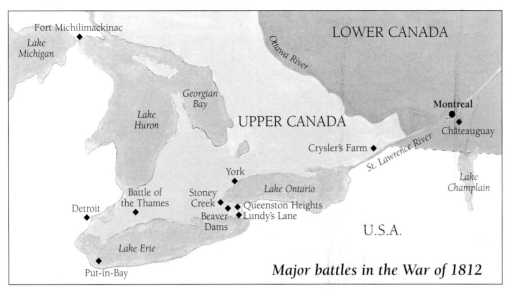

Major battles in the War of 1812

General Isaac Brock

Attack and Defence

The Americans thought it would be easy to conquer Upper and Lower Canada. They expected the settlers to welcome them, eager to get rid of their British rulers. After all, about four-fifths of the people of Upper Canada were American, many of them recent arrivals, and Lower Canada was largely French.

The Americans soon found that they were very unwelcome. As they struggled through the forests, they were ambushed by Aboriginal soldiers. Many Aboriginals, including Tecumseh and his followers, fought for the British, as did militiamen from both Upper and Lower Canada. The militia were regiments of settlers who could be called on to defend the colony in an emergency. However, the core of the army were regular soldiers from Britain.

Major Battles

In Upper Canada, the troops were led by General Isaac Brock, who won three victories early in the war (at Michilimackinac, Detroit and Queenston Heights). But Brock was killed at Queenston Heights. The next year, Tecumseh was killed trying to stop the Americans after British troops had fled. Two great heroes were dead, and Upper Canada mourned — and worried.

During 1813, the Americans often seemed to be winning. Much

of the war was fought on Lakes Erie and Ontario and in the Niagara Peninsula. The Americans had built large warships on the lakes, and they had the upper hand there. They twice captured York, the tiny capital of Upper Canada. But there were British victories at Stoney Creek, Beaver Dams, Crysler's Farm and Lundy's Lane. These battles are part of Canadian folklore because of the role played by the settlers, who were defending their homes and families.

Tecumseh

At Queenston Heights, the Americans attacked across the Niagara River.

Other Heroes of the War

Laura Secord walked 30 km (19 mi.) to give warning of the Americans' planned attack at Beaver Dams. But the heroes of the battle were the Aboriginal troops, who made a surprise attack on the Americans. "Not a shot was fired on our side by any but the Indians," wrote the British officer Lt. James FitzGibbon.

An even more memorable victory took place in Lower Canada, which was invaded in the fall of 1813. At the Châteauguay River, on October 26, a few hundred Canadians under Lt. Col. Charles de Salaberry ambushed 4000 Americans who were planning to attack Montreal. Again, no British troops were involved. This victory was won by Canadians — French speaking, English speaking and Aboriginal — all fighting together in a common cause.

The Battle of Châteauguay.

The War Ends

The war ground to a halt in 1814. By the Treaty of Ghent, the borders stayed the same, but the losers were the Aboriginal people. South of the border, they soon lost their lands to settlers. In the Canadas, they lost their role as allies — they were no longer needed to help defend the colonies, so they had little influence.

If there was a winner, it was Upper and Lower Canada, because people had gained a new outlook. Rather than stressing their ethnic origins, many now thought of themselves as Canadians. The colonies on the Atlantic coast had also gained more sense of identity. Their ships had raided American ships during the war, and Halifax had thrived as an important naval base. Instead of destroying British North America, the War of 1812 set it on course for the future.

DID YOU KNOW

It is because of the War of 1812 that the home of the U.S. president is called the White House. The British invaded Washington in 1814 and burned public buildings, including the president's home. When the damaged part was rebuilt, the outer walls were whitewashed to hide the burn marks.

REBELLIONS OF 1837–38

During the 1820s and 1830s, thousands of British immigrants arrived in Upper and Lower Canada. But there were still far more French than English in Lower Canada. And there were still lots of American-born settlers in Upper Canada.

Many of these people wanted more say in the government. In the United States, Americans elected their leaders. But the only elected body in Upper Canada was the Legislative Assembly, which had very little power. All important decisions were made by the Executive and Legislative Councils, whose members were chosen by the governor. The governor usually chose wealthy Loyalists, such as landowners and businessmen — people who were used to running things.

Problems in Upper Canada

The men who ran Upper Canada were nicknamed the Family Compact, because many of them were related. They worked hard to improve the colony with canals and other large projects. But these benefited the businessmen more than the settlers. "Where are the roads and bridges we need?" asked the settlers. "Where are the schools for our children?"

The settlers had a strong supporter — William Lyon Mackenzie, who ran a newspaper that criticized the Family Compact. Mackenzie was a fiery Scotsman who wore a red wig, which he tore off his head and waved when he got excited. The settlers elected him to the Legislative Assembly, where he tried to get the system of government changed so that elected men would run the colony. Other politicians also were calling for change. These men were known as Reformers.

Mackenzie's enemies called him William Liar Mackenzie because of the rude things he said about them. He was expelled from the Legislative Assembly four times, but each time he was re-elected by the people. In 1834, when York became the city of Toronto, Mackenzie was elected mayor.

Problems in Lower Canada

In Lower Canada, the British governor and his friends were known as the Château Clique. Here, too, the governor and his councils held the power, and their laws benefited businessmen more than ordinary farmers. Most of the Château Clique were British businessmen or wealthy seigneurs.

In contrast, most habitants were desperately poor. Even so, they had to give money to the church and pay rent to the seigneurs. They felt trapped in the seigneurial system (see page 16) and lacked the power to improve their lives.

The members of the Legislative Assembly also wanted more power. Most were well-educated Canadiens who were eager to run things themselves. With both the government and business in the hands of the British, they feared they would lose their French language and culture.

(see page 16)

PROFILE

LOUIS-JOSEPH PAPINEAU

Louis-Joseph Papineau was a seigneur, but he admired the American system of government and wanted something like it for Canadiens. His rousing speeches brought on the rebellion, though he didn't mean to start a revolt. He was simply trying to get the British to make the changes he wanted.

To try to keep their traditions, a group of Canadiens formed the Patriote party. Its chief spokesman in the Assembly was Louis-Joseph Papineau, whose passionate speeches made Canadiens proud of their history. Many Patriotes began to wear homespun clothing like the habitants.

"ALTHOUGH FRENCH IS THE MOST COMMONLY SPOKEN LANGUAGE, MOST NEWSPAPERS … AND EVEN COMMERCIAL SIGNS OF FRENCH MERCHANTS ARE IN ENGLISH."

— *Alexis de Tocqueville, a visitor from France*

Quick Facts
Two Members of the Family Compact

• *John Strachan, Anglican archdeacon of York (later bishop of Toronto), member of both Executive Council (1817–36) and Legislative Council (1820–41).*

• *John Beverley Robinson, chief justice of Upper Canada (1829–41), long-time member of Legislative Council and briefly president of Executive Council. He had been educated at Strachan's private boys' school, and his daughter married Strachan's son.*

Desperate Times

By the 1830s, many habitants were starving. Insects and disease had destroyed their wheat crops. Even in good years, many could barely survive, because their farms had become smaller as each generation divided the land among its children. The habitants needed more land, and they were furious when the government set aside a large area for English farmers. The Patriotes were angry about that, too.

In 1834, the Patriotes drew up a list of demands, and these Ninety-Two Resolutions were sent to Britain. When the British government at last replied in 1837, it made no effort to meet the Patriotes' demands. It said that British immigrants would continue to settle in Lower Canada and the Assembly would not be given any more power.

Rebellion in Lower Canada

In the fall of 1837, desperate habitants roamed the countryside attacking English farms. In November, the trouble spread to Montreal, where groups of young Loyalists clashed with young Patriotes. Alarmed by these riots, the governor ordered the arrest of Patriote leaders.

Papineau had already fled to the village of St-Denis, which was attacked by British soldiers on November 23. Dr. Wolfred Nelson, an English member of the Patriote party, led the Patriote defenders, and they beat off the soldiers. But two days later, another group of Patriotes was defeated at St-Charles.

The third battle of the rebellion took place at the village of St-Eustache on December 14. The Patriotes had taken up their position inside a church, which British soldiers set alight. As the Patriotes ran from the flaming building, they were shot by the soldiers (above). About 70 Patriotes died. During the next few weeks, others were hunted down and imprisoned. Papineau escaped to the United States, but other leaders were caught, including Nelson.

Rebellion in Upper Canada

The fighting in Lower Canada spurred Mackenzie to action. By 1837, he had given up all hope of achieving change peacefully. He was now urging settlers to throw out the British and make Upper Canada independent like

"THE TIME HAS COME TO MELT OUR SPOONS INTO BULLETS!"

Wolfred Nelson

the United States. But most British settlers wanted to stay British. Only a few hundred farmers answered Mackenzie's call to rebel.

They gathered at Montgomery's Tavern, north of Toronto, and on December 5 they marched down Yonge Street. On the way, they were ambushed by a small group of militiamen, who easily scattered the poorly armed farmers. Two days later, a large column of Loyalists, led by bands and bagpipers, marched north to meet the rebels. In the brief battle, most of the rebels fled, though Mackenzie screamed at them to stay and fight.

Mackenzie escaped to the United States and then made his base on Navy Island in the Niagara River. From there he planned to invade Upper Canada, but his enemies

and French. Since Durham viewed Canadiens as a backward people without history or literature, he suggested that the two Canadas should be united so that the French would eventually be assimilated by the English. He also suggested a system of "responsible government" that would give power to the elected Assembly.

In 1841, Upper Canada was renamed Canada West, and Lower Canada became Canada East. Together, they formed a colony called the Province of Canada. Both Canadas elected the same number of members to a single Assembly. After a pardon allowed rebels to return, Papineau, Mackenzie and Nelson all became members of the Assembly.

attacked first. The ship *Caroline*, which supplied Mackenzie with food and arms, was boarded by Loyalists, who set it on fire and sent it plunging over Niagara Falls (above). Mackenzie had to leave the island, though he still hoped to persuade Americans to help him "free" Upper Canada. However, the U.S. government saw him as a troublemaker and imprisoned him for almost a year.

The Results

In 1838, groups of rebels and their American supporters made several raids into Upper Canada, but they were driven back. A rising in Lower Canada was also put down easily, and hundreds of Patriotes were thrown in jail. Most were later released, but 12 were hanged and 58 were sent as convicts to Australia. In Upper Canada, two were hanged and 24 sent to Australia.

In the meantime, the British government had sent Lord Durham to Canada to look into the causes of the rebellions. He concluded that the main problem was between English

Responsible Government

Under responsible government, the governor could no longer choose the members of the Executive Council. He had to appoint the leaders of the party that had most members elected to the Legislative Assembly. This meant that the colony was at last governed by politicians elected by the people. If the Executive did something unpopular and was outvoted in the Assembly, it had to resign and a new election was held. Basically, Canada still has this system today.

The first colony in the British Empire to have responsible government was Nova Scotia, where the popular journalist and politician Joseph Howe had long been calling for it. The event occurred in February 1848, after James Boyle Uniacke and his fellow Reformers won the Nova Scotia election.

The next to get responsible government was the Province of Canada, in March 1848, under Reform leaders Louis-Hippolyte LaFontaine and Robert Baldwin. The other colonies of British North America soon followed — Prince Edward Island in 1851, New Brunswick in 1854 and Newfoundland in 1855. (See also Representative Government on page 27.)

Joseph Howe

Louis-Hippolyte LaFontaine

Robert Baldwin

LIFE AT MID-CENTURY

The 1840s to 1860s were exciting years, when new machines and other inventions brought great changes to the way people lived and worked. Many of the immigrants who arrived chose to get jobs in the cities rather than becoming settlers. Montreal, the largest city, had about 50 000 inhabitants by 1850. Toronto was growing fast, and so were Halifax and other towns on the east coast.

On the west coast, the colony of Vancouver Island was formed in 1849. It was run by the Hudson's Bay Company, and its few settlers were HBC men and their families. Most of them farmed near Fort Victoria, which the HBC had built in 1843 as its Pacific headquarters.

The Grand Trunk Railway in the Province of Canada was the world's longest railway when it was built in the 1850s.

The Gold Rush

Victoria remained a quiet little village until April 1858, when a ship arrived from California packed with 400 excited men — more than the entire population of Victoria! The men had heard that gold had been found on the Fraser River, and they'd come to Victoria to get supplies before sailing across to the mainland.

By June, more than 10 000 gold seekers had passed through Victoria, which quickly grew into a city. Most miners were Americans, and this worried Vancouver Island's governor, James Douglas. With so many Americans searching for gold on the mainland, he feared the United States might claim the territory. Although it was part of the HBC lands, the only British living there were a few fur-trading families. It could easily be taken over, like the Oregon Territory (see page 41).

Aboriginal Lands

Governor Douglas, whose wife was Métis, tried to see that any land needed for settlers was bought from the Aboriginal owners, not just taken. But after Douglas retired, the colonists said that Aboriginal land was "unoccupied" unless it contained houses or fenced farmland. Vast areas of British Columbia were taken from the First Nations without any treaty or payment. That's why there are so many land claims in British Columbia today, as First Nations try to get back their lands (see, for example, the Nisga'a Treaty, page 68).

The Gold Miners

Many of the miners were rough, lawless people, so Governor Douglas took quick action to control them. To stress that they were on British territory, he made them get a licence from him and obey British laws. Meanwhile, in 1858, Britain formed the colony of British Columbia on the mainland. This name was kept when British Columbia and Vancouver Island became one single colony in 1866.

By then, a gold rush in the Cariboo Mountains had brought many more people to the area. One of the most famous was Billy Barker, who dug up $1000 worth of gold in two days. He and his partners eventually made $600 000. Most people didn't make nearly so much, but many stayed on to farm or start businesses.

The Underground Railroad

After 1834, when slavery was ended in the British Empire, thousands of American slaves fled north to the British colonies. The secret network of people who helped them on their journey was known as a "railroad." Harriet Tubman, a slave who escaped to Canada West, risked her life time and again by going back to the American South to bring others to safety.

The Prairies

Everything east of British Columbia as far as the Province of Canada was HBC territory. Scattered throughout this area were a few trading forts, but the only settlement was at Red River. The HBC didn't allow settlers anywhere else. The fur trade worked best when Aboriginal people had space to live their own lives, whether trapping beaver in the forests or hunting buffalo on the prairies.

Now that the Plains nations had guns and horses, buffalo hunting was much easier, though it was still very dangerous. The hunters galloped full tilt among the herds as the terrified beasts thundered across the prairie. The Métis of the Red River region came together twice a year for huge buffalo hunts. These hunts were highly organized, with hunt captains and special rules and customs. The hunts and their traditions caused the Métis to think of themselves as a separate nation, different from other people.

There were several thousand Métis living in the Red River Settlement (above). As well, missionaries had come and built churches and schools — Protestant for the English speakers and Catholic for the French. The majority of Métis were French-speaking Catholics.

A Flood of British Immigrants

Most English-speaking people were Protestant, though many Irish were Catholic. Each year, thousands of Irish, Scots and English arrived in British North America. Most headed for the Province of Canada, though some chose Nova Scotia or New Brunswick.

Very few immigrants went to Prince Edward Island. Although it had good farmland, most of the island was owned by people who lived in Britain, so settlers had to rent their farms. Newfoundland didn't attract many immigrants either. It was too rocky for successful farming, but some Irish came to join the English in the fishery. Fishing was important to all the Atlantic colonies and was the main form of work in Newfoundland.

A flood of Irish arrived in all the colonies in the late 1840s, fleeing from a terrible famine. Many people in Ireland were so poor that they lived entirely on potatoes. When the potato crop was killed by a disease, they had nothing to eat. Crammed into ships, hundreds of thousands of Irish headed for North America.

Most were sick or weak, and many died on the way. The survivors went mainly to the cities in search of jobs.

The Growth of Industries

Some of the immigrants became labourers, building new roads and canals. Others found work in the timber trade, which was a major industry in New Brunswick and the Ottawa valley. In winter, loggers lived in bunkhouses in the woods while they cut down the huge trees. In spring, they tied the logs together to make rafts, which they floated down the rivers.

Some of the wood was made into ships in Quebec or the Maritime ports, but much of it was exported to Britain. Many of the Royal Navy's ships had masts made from pine trees grown in British North America. Wheat, coal, fish and other raw materials also were exported to Britain. These exports brought money to the colonies and helped pay for costly projects, such as railways and canals.

The Railway Age

Canada's first railway was opened in 1836. It was 23 km (14 mi.) long, running between the St. Lawrence and Richelieu rivers. Four years later, a 9.5 km (6 mi.) railway was built in Nova Scotia. Longer railways soon followed. By 1860, various railway companies had built more than 3200 km (1988 mi.) of track.

The railways were a great help to business because they could transport goods quickly, so that something grown in Canada West could be sold as far away as Quebec City. Some railways took goods to the United States, which in 1854 signed the Reciprocity Treaty to make trade easier with the British colonies.

Because of these new markets, it was worth making a greater number of goods than were needed locally. So businessmen started factories to make shoes, tools — all sorts of things. Like the trains, the factories were powered by steam engines. And, of course, they provided people with jobs.

Exciting Times

The railways had a huge effect on people's lives. For instance, a family used to take days to travel from Chatham to Toronto, jolting across bumpy dirt roads in a horse-drawn stagecoach. Now they could do the journey in a few hours. Mail also could now be delivered more quickly.

Engineers and scientists played a big part in the new developments. After the Americans invented the telegraph, Canadian engineers built telegraph lines linking the main cities. In 1866, an underwater telegraph cable was laid all the way across the Atlantic, from Ireland to Newfoundland. North America could now get instant news from Europe.

In the major cities, streets and public buildings were lit by gaslight, though most homes still used candles or whale-oil lamps (which smelled horrible). Kerosene lamps first came into use in the late 1850s after a Nova Scotian, Abraham Gesner, found a way of refining crude oil to make kerosene. This new use for oil caused people to search for it. The first oil well in North America was dug near Petrolia, Canada West, by James Miller Williams in 1857.

DID YOU KNOW

The sailing ship *Marco Polo*, built at Saint John, New Brunswick, in 1851, was the fastest ship in the world at the time.

DID YOU KNOW

The U.S. states of Oregon and Washington might today be part of Canada if things had gone differently. This area between the Columbia River and the 49th parallel was called the Oregon Territory and was part of the HBC's fur-trading lands. But the HBC's chief man in Oregon allowed so many Americans to settle there that the United States claimed the territory. In 1846, to avoid a war, Britain agreed that the United States could have the Oregon Territory.

CONFEDERATION

By the 1860s, the British North American colonies were no longer important trading partners of Britain. Yet Britain still had to look after them and send troops to defend them. This cost a lot of money. So the British were pleased when people in the colonies talked of uniting to form a country.

As one country, the former colonies could be linked with railways to help trade between them. This was important because the United States wanted to end the Reciprocity Treaty of 1854 (page 41). As well, union would help the colonies resist any takeover by the United States. American settlers wanted to move north into the unsettled HBC lands on the prairies. If the new country bought the HBC lands, it could settle Canadians there.

The Fathers of Confederation.

Trouble in the Canadas

George Brown, owner of the *Globe* newspaper, dreamed of Canada becoming a great nation stretching from sea to sea. Brown was a leading politician in Canada West. The other main leader there was his bitter enemy, John A. Macdonald. Macdonald was a Tory (like today's Conservatives) while Brown was leader of the Clear Grits — an offshoot of the Reformers (which became the Liberals).

In the Legislative Assembly, the Grits and Reformers were allies of the *Rouge* party of Canada East, while the Tories and *Bleus* were partners. But the allies didn't always vote the same way. Now that Canada West had more people than Canada East, the Reformers wanted "rep by pop" (representation by population), which meant that the number of seats in the Assembly would be based on the size of the population. Neither the *Rouges* nor the *Bleus* wanted that. It would give English Canadians so many seats that they could do whatever they wanted.

With so many parties wanting different things, no government stayed in power for long, so hardly any laws got passed. Clearly, something had to be done.

The Great Coalition

It was Brown who eventually broke the log-jam. In 1864, he asked Macdonald to join him in forming a coalition (joint) government to arrange a union with other colonies. Macdonald took up the idea and agreed to work with Brown. So did the *Bleu* leader, George-Étienne Cartier.

The Maritime colonies were already thinking of a union of their own and planned to meet in Charlottetown in September 1864. The Canadians asked if they could come, too. They went there by ship, because there was no rail link. During the meetings, the politicians

Charles Tupper (top left) was Nova Scotia's leading Father of Confederation — and a future prime minister

George-Étienne Cartier (bottom left), a former Patriote, persuaded many people in Canada East to support Confederation.

George Brown's (centre) vision of Canada got the Confederation movement rolling.

Irish-born Thomas D'Arcy McGee (top right) was a brilliant speaker and one of the most enthusiastic promoters of Confederation.

Samuel Leonard Tilley (bottom right) of New Brunswick suggested Canada's title, "dominion," and its motto, "a mari usque ad mare" (which means "from sea to sea").

agreed that an Intercolonial Railway would be built to connect the Maritimes with Canada.

In October, a second conference was held in Quebec City to work out the details. Canada was to have a federal (national) government to handle nationwide matters, such as defence and trade. As well, each province would have its own government to make laws about local and cultural matters, such as language and education within the province.

PROFILE

JOHN A. MACDONALD

John A. Macdonald was the leading Father of Confederation. He was very skilful at getting people to agree despite their different views. He played a major role in working out the details of Confederation and became Canada's first prime minister. Later, he helped build Canada into a nation that stretched from the Atlantic to the Pacific Ocean.

Against Confederation

Both Newfoundland and Prince Edward Island decided not to join the union. Under "rep by pop," they would have very few seats in the federal parliament, so would have little say. Nova Scotia and New Brunswick had similar fears, but eventually agreed to the scheme (though some of their people still opposed it — especially Nova Scotian Joseph Howe).

In Canada East, many people hated the plan, even though their province, Quebec, would control education, language and religion. They thought the federal government was being made too strong. The provinces should have control of many more things, they said. This was particularly important for Quebec, because the federal parliament would have more English-speaking than French-speaking members. So its laws might pay little attention to Canadien needs.

To make Confederation more appealing, Quebec was promised it would never have fewer than 65 seats in the federal parliament, even if its population decreased. The other provinces were to have "rep by pop" — Ontario, 82 seats, Nova Scotia, 19, New Brunswick, 15.

Full Steam Ahead

While Canadians were discussing union, the Americans were fighting a civil war in which Britain helped the south. After the north won in 1865, many Americans wanted to hit back by invading the British colonies. When some Irish Americans, called Fenians, launched raids across the border, Canadians feared a major invasion. This made them realize that they needed to unite to protect themselves. So with the majority now in favour, a conference was held in England in 1866 to make the final arrangements.

In 1867, the British North America Act was passed, and on July 1, Canada was born (below). Made up of four provinces — Ontario, Quebec, New Brunswick and Nova Scotia — it was a self-governing nation within the British Empire. Only a few things, such as relations with other countries, would still be decided by Britain.

THE RED RIVER RISING

Two years later, Canada faced a crisis. The federal government had arranged to buy the Hudson's Bay Company territories, but it hadn't consulted the people who lived there. When the Métis heard of the plan, they were very upset. Already, some Protestants from Ontario had moved to the Red River, and they boasted that when the region became part of Canada, settlers would take over Métis farms.

In 1869, a team of surveyors arrived to mark off land for the settlers. Only unoccupied land was meant to be measured, but the team didn't understand the Métis landholding system. In October, while surveying on Métis land, they were stopped by a group of angry Métis led by 24-year-old Louis Riel.

Riel Takes Charge

Riel was better educated than most Métis — he had gone to college in Montreal. Soon the Métis began to look on him as their leader. In November 1869, Riel and a group of armed Métis seized Upper Fort Garry, the HBC's main base at Red River. Meanwhile, another group had stopped the new governor from entering the settlement. The Métis didn't see why they should have a Canadian governor until the land sale actually took place.

The Métis then formed a "provisional" (temporary) government and drew up a List of Rights to make sure that their lands, customs and religion would be protected. The list included a demand to have their own province, where French as well as English would be used in the legislature and courts. Early in 1870, three men set off for Ottawa to give the list to the federal government.

The HBC sale affected Aboriginal people as well as Métis. They, too, had no say in laws about them, and in 1869 the Indian Act took away the right of Aboriginal communities to govern themselves.

"WE MUST MAKE CANADA RESPECT US."

Louis Riel

More Trouble

Everything might have gone smoothly if it hadn't been for the Canadian newcomers at Red River. Many of them refused to obey Riel's "provisional government."

In February, a group of Canadians set out to capture Upper Fort Garry — but instead were captured by the Métis. Among the captives was Thomas Scott, a young tough from Ontario who fought and insulted his guards. He caused so much trouble that the Métis put him on trial and found him guilty of "insubordination." By the rules of the buffalo hunt, this type of disobedience was punished by death. Scott was shot the next day.

The news of Scott's death caused an uproar when it reached Ontario. English Canadians wanted revenge, and they saw no reason why they should agree to the Métis List of Rights. Despite this, the federal government passed the Manitoba Act, giving the Métis most of the things they wanted. The Act said that the Red River area would become a province called Manitoba on July 15, 1870.

The Red River Expedition

While the people at Red River were waiting for Manitoba's birth, they were also waiting nervously for an army to arrive. Against the wishes of most French Canadians, a force of regular soldiers and militiamen had been sent west to restore order at Red River (below). Hundreds of English Canadians had joined the militia, intent on punishing the Métis for the "murder" of Scott.

The expedition included 400 voyageurs, many of whom were Iroquois. They paddled the boats that took the troops along the western waterways. There was no railway west of Lake Superior, and sometimes the men had to go overland — carrying their boats and all their supplies.

They took more than three months to reach the Red River. When they arrived in August, Manitoba was already a province and all was peaceful in the settlement. Not for long. The militiamen were still eager to avenge Scott's death. They beat up many of the Métis and killed two of them, though Riel escaped. He slipped across the border into the United States.

Métis Move Farther West

The Manitoba Act had given the Métis their province, but they were soon outnumbered by new settlers. Many of the Métis lost their land to settlers, because they couldn't prove that they owned their farms. The government gave these Métis "scrip" — a piece of paper that could be exchanged for a plot of land somewhere else. But land-hungry newcomers persuaded many of the Métis to sell their scrip, often for very little money. During the next few years, about half the Métis left Manitoba. Most moved west to what is now Saskatchewan.

DID YOU KNOW

Colonel Wolseley, the British soldier who led the Red River Expedition, called the Iroquois "the most daring and skilful of all Canadian voyageurs." He later hired some of them to take an expedition up the Nile River in Egypt.

FROM SEA TO SEA

One year after Manitoba joined Canada, British Columbia did, too — but on condition that it was connected to Canada by rail. That meant building a railway through the Rocky Mountains, which some people thought impossible. Even so, the federal government promised to build the line within ten years.

Prince Edward Island also wanted a railway and had gone into debt building one. Its main industry — making wooden ships — wasn't bringing in much money, because many ships now had iron hulls. As well, much of P.E.I. was still owned by people in Britain. Canada offered to help buy the land as well as paying the railway debts. In return, Prince Edward Island joined Canada in 1873.

By the 1870s, many Canadians lived in cities.

A Growing Nation

The federal government helped British Columbia and P.E.I. join Confederation because bigger meant stronger — and not only against the United States. Canada was stronger because it now had 4 million people contributing in many ways.

Among them was Adolphe-Basile Routhier, author of the lyrics to "O Canada!" (which he wrote in French), and Calixa Lavallée, who wrote the music. There were artists and poets, scientists and inventors — including Alexander Graham Bell, who invented the telephone in 1876. Meanwhile, women were taking on new roles, doing work that was normally done by men.

Calixa Lavallée

Child Workers

In spite of the Schools Acts, many children from poor families worked in factories instead of going to school. Some worked 60 hours a week for only a dollar a week. Yet that dollar helped the family survive.

The National Policy

John A. Macdonald's attempts to build a railway across Canada landed him in trouble. He promised to give the job to Sir Hugh Allan — the same man who gave $350 000 to Macdonald and other Conservatives to help them win the 1872 election. Macdonald was accused of accepting bribes and had to resign. Alexander Mackenzie then became prime minister.

Macdonald was so disgraced that people thought his career was finished. But he was back as prime minister in 1878, thanks to his National Policy. This policy involved charging low taxes on imported raw materials (such as unprocessed cotton) but high taxes on factory-made goods (such as cotton cloth). The aim was to help Canadian business by stopping cheap American goods from pouring into Canada.

The policy was very successful. New factories were started to make printed cotton, clocks, knives and forks — all sorts of things that used to be imported. Unskilled women could get work in these factories.

Ice hockey was invented in Canada. The first organized game was played in 1875 after a student at McGill University made a list of rules.

Women at Work

Many women became teachers after 1871, when the Ontario Schools Act said that all children between the ages of 7 and 12 must attend school. This Act set the pattern for the public school system in other provinces. With so many children going to school, many new teachers were needed.

It was hard for women to qualify in other professions, because no Canadian university accepted women students. The first was Mount Allison in New Brunswick, where in 1875 Grace Lockhart became the first woman to get a degree in Canada. Women who wanted to be doctors had to graduate in the United States, like Emily Stowe (in 1867) and Jennie Trout (in 1875). The first woman to earn a medical degree in Canada was Stowe's daughter, Augusta Stowe-Gullen (in 1883).

Like early women doctors, women who wanted to be lawyers faced great opposition. The first was Clara Brett Martin (called to the bar in 1897).

Factory owners liked to employ women because they could be paid less than men.

The Canadian Pacific Railway

Thousands of men were needed as labourers once building started on the railway to the Pacific. Little progress had been made while Mackenzie was prime minister, but under Macdonald things got moving at last.

A new Canadian Pacific Railway Company was formed in 1881 (the year the government had promised to complete the line), and William Van Horne was appointed general manager. Somehow, Van Horne had to build a railway through the rock of the Canadian Shield north of Lake Superior, then across the vast prairies, and finally through the Rockies. He said he could do it.

Prime Ministers' Timeline

Sir John A. Macdonald, 1867–73 (Conservative, called Liberal-Conservative)

Alexander Mackenzie, 1873–78 (Liberal)

Macdonald, 1878–91 (Conservative)

THE GREAT NORTH-WEST

The land bought from the HBC in 1870 stretched north into the Arctic and west across the prairies to the border of British Columbia. The whole region, except for Manitoba, was called the North-West Territories.

Very few settlers lived there before the railway was built. On the prairies, the Plains people still lived much as they had always done, hunting buffalo across open country. But in the early 1870s, American traders moved onto the Canadian prairies, where they built forts and traded whisky for furs. There was nobody to stop them now that the HBC wasn't in charge of the region. Soon the prairies became as wild and lawless as the American West.

The Mounties

To restore order, the government created the North-West Mounted Police (right). They arrived on the western prairies in 1874, having marched 1300 km (810 mi.) across the plains. Although weary after their long journey, they quickly established Canadian law and stopped the whisky trade.

Most Aboriginal people were pleased with the Mounties, who tried to act very fairly. Their officer, Colonel James Macleod, often consulted with the chiefs when deciding what punishment to give to someone who had broken a law.

Trouble in the North-West

On their march west, the police had seen huge herds of buffalo. Six years later, hardly any were left. As the herds dwindled, the Plains people began to starve. They had little choice when the government said that if they gave up their land it would feed and educate them. So they signed treaties and went to live on reserves.

The Plains people were miserable there — bossed around by government agents, who kept them short of food. The Métis in the Saskatchewan valley were also unhappy. New settlers were moving onto their land, just as people had at the Red River. The

Métis complained to the government, but nothing was done.

In 1884, the Métis asked Louis Riel to come and help them. But even he couldn't get the government to take notice. So in March 1885 he formed another provisional government. Soon afterwards, a group of Métis and Cree fought with police near Duck Lake. Men on both sides were killed before the police retreated.

DID YOU KNOW

In the 1870s, millions of buffalo were killed so that their hides could be made into belts to drive factory machinery. A new type of rifle made it easy to kill a lot of buffalo very quickly.

Trials and Punishments

Eight Aboriginal people were hanged for their part in the rebellion. Others were imprisoned, including Big Bear and another Cree chief, Poundmaker. In fact, all the Plains people suffered. Life on the reserves became even worse, and all traditions were banned.

Meanwhile, Louis Riel was tried and found guilty of treason. His trial divided Canada. French Canadians saw Riel as a hero and wanted him pardoned. But English Canadians wanted him hanged as a murderer. Prime Minister Macdonald gave in to the English, and Riel was hanged in November 1885.

The Northwest Rebellion of 1885

The news of the Duck Lake battle caused panic among the settlers, and many fled for safety to the police fort at Battleford. As the panic spread, a few Aboriginal people attacked the hated government agents. The worst incident was at Frog Lake, where some Cree killed nine men, including two priests.

Most Aboriginal people didn't join the uprising. They realized it would do no good. Yet rumours spread to eastern Canada that all the West was in turmoil and every settler in danger. Volunteers rushed to join the militia. Because the railway was almost finished, the troops could be sped west. But several months passed before the rebellion was over. In May, the Métis made a valiant last stand at their settlement of Batoche. Afterwards, Riel surrendered. But a Cree chief, Big Bear, held out until July.

Gabriel Dumont, a former leader of the buffalo hunt, was the Métis military leader during the rebellion.

The Canadian Pacific Railway

Surveyors and engineers as well as thousands of labourers worked on the railway. After William Van Horne took charge of construction in January 1882, the track was laid at an amazing rate. The line across the prairies reached Calgary in 1883. Wherever it went, people flooded in to start businesses. Winnipeg was already a boom town.

Work was slower and far more difficult in the Rocky Mountains and in the Shield north of Lake Superior. Here, tunnels had to be blasted through the rock and bridges built across deep gorges. Much of this dangerous work was done by labourers brought from China. The line was completed in November 1885, and the first passenger train to cross Canada arrived on the Pacific coast in July 1886.

A NEW ERA

In 1896, Sir Wilfrid Laurier became prime minister. Hoping to fill the West with people, his government advertised throughout Europe, promising good farmland and great opportunities. Settlers poured in — from Ukraine, Poland, Germany, Norway and many other places.

Some got a horrible shock when they saw where they were to live. It was just a flat stretch of prairie — nothing except grass as far as the horizon. A settler's first home was often a flimsy shack or a sod house made of turf. But farms and ranches were soon started, and towns grew up to supply them.

WILFRID LAURIER

Sir Wilfrid Laurier was Canada's first French-Canadian prime minister. A brilliant speaker in both languages, he tried to please both French and English Canada. English Canadians wanted him to help Britain in the South African War (Boer War) of 1899–1902, but most French Canadians didn't want to get involved in Britain's wars. Eventually, Laurier sent only volunteers to South Africa. He also found a compromise in the Manitoba Schools Question (about separate Catholic schools).

The Booming West

In 1905, the provinces of Alberta and Saskatchewan were formed. Both soon had a network of railways to take wheat and other products to distant markets. So much wheat was grown that Canada was called "the breadbasket of the world."

The wheat boom was the result of two Canadian developments — new types of farm machinery and a new strain of wheat. Much of the machinery was made by Massey-Harris, the largest farm-equipment company in the British Empire. The wheat was called Marquis and had been bred by Charles Saunders. It did well on the prairies because it ripened faster than other wheats.

Women Demand the Vote

By the turn of the century, women were taking a bigger part in public life. Many belonged to the temperance movement, which wanted liquor banned. Some visited factories to get working conditions improved. Many were members of the suffrage movement, which aimed to get women the vote. Only men could vote, though some women had voted in Lower Canada until an 1834 law stopped them.

The suffrage movement was especially strong on the prairies, where Nellie McClung was a leading activist. The prairie provinces were the first to give women the vote, beginning with Manitoba in January 1916. By the end of World War I, women also had the right to vote in federal elections.

World War I (1914–18)

When Britain declared war on Germany in 1914, Canada went to war, too. The country was divided between those who were eager to support Britain and those who were opposed. Most French Canadians were furious when in 1917 Prime Minister Borden passed a conscription law (a

The Klondike Gold Rush

During the Klondike gold rush of 1897–99, more than 100 000 gold seekers flocked to the Yukon, scaling dangerous mountain passes to get there. Because of all these people, the Yukon was made a separate territory in 1898. The rest of the old North-West was renamed the Northwest Territories.

Quick Facts
Women Get the Vote

• *In provincial elections: Manitoba, Saskatchewan, Alberta (1916); British Columbia, Ontario (1917); Nova Scotia (1918); New Brunswick (1919); Prince Edward Island (1922); Newfoundland (1925); Quebec (1940)*

• *In federal elections: 1918*

---

law to make men join the armed forces). Henri Bourassa — a passionate champion of French Canada — expressed many Quebeckers' feelings as he attacked the government in his newspaper *Le Devoir*.

Most of the war's battles took place in France, which was one of Canada's allies. But thousands of people were killed or blinded in Canada when a ship of explosives blew up in Halifax harbour.

Meanwhile, soldiers wrote home with horrible stories about the battlefields of France, where they lived in muddy trenches and died by the thousand.

In the battle of Vimy Ridge during Easter 1917, over 10 000 Canadians were killed or wounded. Yet Vimy gave Canada a great sense of pride because the victory was won entirely by the Canadian Corps, without any other nations helping. The war ended the following year when Germany surrendered.

DID YOU KNOW

In 1915, John McCrae of Guelph, Ontario, wrote the famous poem "In Flanders Fields" while he was serving in France. He died in the last year of the war.

Prime Ministers' Timeline

Sir John Abbott, 1891–92 (Conservative)	*Sir John Thompson, 1892–94 (Conservative)*	*Sir Mackenzie Bowell, 1894–96 (Conservative)*	*Sir Charles Tupper, May–July 1896 (Conservative)*	*Sir Wilfrid Laurier, 1896–1911 (Liberal)*	*Sir Robert Borden, 1911–20 (Conservative and Union)*

CHANGING TIMES

anada had changed a lot since the beginning of the century. By 1920, factories and city homes had electricity. Many cities had movie houses where people watched silent films. Thousands of Canadians owned "motor cars," and much of the farm machinery also was motor driven.

A few people even owned airplanes. Some of the most famous air aces of World War I had been Canadians. After the war, a large number of them became bush pilots, flying over rugged country. They took passengers, goods and mail to remote parts of the West and North.

The Winnipeg General Strike brought the city to a halt.

Unions and Strikes

There were many Canadians who didn't benefit from the good times. Across the country, workers in factories and mines still laboured long hours for tiny wages. Since the late nineteenth century, groups of workers had formed unions to try and get better conditions. But this angered their employers, who called out the police when workers dared to go on strike.

The Winnipeg General Strike of 1919 was brutally put down, as were the 1920s coal-mining strikes in Nova Scotia. Yet the union movement continued to grow.

The Coming of Radio

Quebec-born Reginald Fessenden (left) discovered how to send words and music by radio waves and in 1906 made the world's first public broadcast. By the 1920s, Canada had several small radio stations, and in 1936 the Canadian Broadcasting Corporation (CBC) was formed. The CBC was heard from coast to coast, bringing Canadians together in a way that hadn't been possible before.

DID YOU KNOW

In 1921, Frederick Banting and Charles Best discovered how to produce a drug called insulin, which prevented people from dying of diabetes.

The Statute of Westminster of 1931

The Statute of Westminster of 1931 said that Canada and other self-governing dominions in the British Commonwealth were equal partners with Great Britain and had the right to make their own laws. Canada had been making its own laws for years, but until 1923 Britain generally had a say in Canada's relations with other countries. Canada now had the right to manage its own affairs, abroad as well as at home.

The Great Depression

Things got worse after 1929, with the beginning of the economic crisis known as the Great Depression. Throughout the world, banks lost money, factories and businesses closed, and millions of people lost their jobs. Farmers on the Canadian prairies got hardly any money for their wheat. Worse still, so little rain fell during the 1930s that many farmers couldn't grow any crops. Their fields turned into clouds of blowing dust.

Unable to afford gasoline, some people used farm animals to pull their cars. They called these vehicles "Bennett buggies," blaming Prime Minister R.B. Bennett for their poverty. He spent large sums trying to end the Depression. But with so many people out of work, Bennett couldn't solve the problem. Neither could the next prime minister, W.L. Mackenzie King.

Aboriginal Activists

Some Aboriginal groups formed organizations to get more rights and to regain land taken from them illegally. One of their leaders was Frederick Ogilvie Loft, who had fought for Britain during the war. In 1918, he formed the League of Indians of Canada.

Loft wanted First Nations to have more say in many areas, including education. Children on reserves spent most of each year away from home in residential schools (above), where they were punished if they spoke their own language or did anything traditional. The aim was to assimilate them, making them like English Canadians. In those days,

many people thought this a good thing to do. But Aboriginal people were strongly against it.

Newfoundland

Even in good times, most Newfoundlanders were desperately poor, living in isolated fishing villages. A missionary doctor, Wilfred Grenfell, had brought some improvement by starting small crafts industries.

Logging and mining also provided jobs. But everything slumped during the Depression, because other countries stopped buying most of Newfoundland's goods.

Newfoundland was still separate from Canada, and it became so deeply in debt that it had to ask Britain for help. So in 1934, Britain set up a "Commission of Government." This was a group of appointed men who were to govern Newfoundland until it could support itself again.

The Famous Five
In 1929, Emily Murphy (right) and her four colleagues (left to right) Nellie McClung, Irene Parlby, Louise McKinney and Henrietta

Muir Edwards won the Persons Case, which legally recognized women as "persons." This meant that women had the right to be senators, judges, and so on.

DID YOU KNOW

Making and selling alcohol was banned in most provinces during much of the 1920s because of laws passed during the war. This ban was called Prohibition.

The Group of Seven

Canada's famous landscape painters, the Group of Seven, held their first exhibition in 1920. The seven artists were Franklin Carmichael, Lawren Harris, A.Y. Jackson, Frank (later Franz) Johnston, Arthur Lismer, J.E.H. MacDonald and F.H. Varley.

Prime Ministers' Timeline

Arthur Meighen, 1920–21 (Conservative)	*William Lyon Mackenzie King, 1921–26 (Liberal)*	*Meighen, June–Sept. 1926 (Conservative)*	*King, 1926–30 (Liberal)*	*Richard Bedford Bennett, 1930–35 (Conservative)*	*King, 1935–48 (Liberal)*

WORLD WAR II

During the late 1930s, Canadians watched anxiously as Germany, under Adolf Hitler, grew stronger and more aggressive. When Hitler's troops invaded Poland in September 1939, Britain and France declared war on Germany. Canada's prime minister, Mackenzie King, waited a week before doing the same — he wanted to show that Canada would make its own decisions.

Most other countries soon joined the conflict, in which the Axis nations (led by Germany, Italy and Japan) fought the Allies (led by Britain, the United States and the Soviet Union). The United States entered the war in December 1941 after its fleet was attacked by the Japanese at Pearl Harbor in Hawaii. Canada then also declared war on Japan.

Canada's Asians

Some of the first Canadians to suffer in the war were troops in Hong Kong, who were killed or taken prisoner when Japan invaded the British colony in 1941. But many people back in Canada also suffered, just because they were of Japanese origin.

By the 1940s, thousands of Asians were living in Canada, mostly in British Columbia. The majority were Chinese, descendants of the railway builders of the 1880s. Others were from Japan or India. Asians were disliked by a lot of Canadians because they were considered "different." They could get only low-paying jobs, and laws had been passed over the years to stop most Asians from coming to Canada.

When Japan entered the war, Japanese Canadians were seen as possible enemies, even though many had been born in Canada and were Canadian citizens. In 1942, more than 20 000 Japanese Canadians were forced out of their homes on the west coast. Their fishing ships and other possessions were sold for very little money, which many of them never received. The men were sent to work in the eastern provinces, while the women and children went to prison camps in the mountains. Although they were not mistreated in the camps, life was very uncomfortable.

The Role of Canadians

As in World War I, thousands of Canadians volunteered to serve in the armed forces, including many French Canadians. Women as well as men joined the forces, which they had not been able to do in 1914, when only nurses had been accepted for service.

Recalling the trouble over conscription (page 52) in the

More than 45 000 women served in the forces, but not as fighters. Most did office work or nursing.

The Holocaust

Adolf Hitler, Germany's leader from 1933 to 1945, told Germans they were members of a superior race. He aimed to purify the race by getting rid of Jews and other people he didn't like. Hitler got rid of them by placing them in concentration camps, where they died of hunger and ill treatment or were killed in gas chambers.

By 1945, six million Jews, many of them children, had been killed. This mass slaughter of Jews is called the Holocaust. Some European Jews who survived the Holocaust settled in Canada after the war.

Newfoundland in War and Peace

In Newfoundland, as in Canada, the war ended the Depression because suddenly there was work for everyone. American and Canadian bases were established in Newfoundland — the part of North America nearest Europe. The bases provided countless jobs for local people. So did Gander, which became a major airport. American-made planes were flown to Britain from there.

Joey Smallwood

After the war, Newfoundlanders were eager to disband the Commission of Government (page 55) and govern themselves. But how? Should Newfoundland become a separate nation? Or join the United States? Or join Canada?

The pro-Canada campaign was led by Joseph ("Joey") Smallwood, a former radio broadcaster and union organizer. Largely because of his efforts, a slim majority of Newfoundlanders voted to join Canada, and Newfoundland became the nation's tenth province on March 31, 1949.

Smallwood became the new province's first premier and he remained in office for the next 23 years. During those years, he tried to make life better for Newfoundlanders — for instance, by launching huge mining and hydroelectric projects to provide more people with work.

Thousands of Canadians took part in D-Day — June 6, 1944 — when the Allies invaded Europe to free it from the Germans.

By the end of the war, more than 42 000 Canadians had lost their lives. Many died fighting to free the Dutch during the final battles in Europe. The war ended when the Axis nations surrendered in 1945.

Mackenzie King

previous war, Mackenzie King put off introducing it for overseas service until late 1944. By then, more troops were urgently needed. More than 900 Canadians had been killed in a disastrous 1942 raid on Dieppe, France. Many others had died in the spring and summer of 1944, during battles in Italy and France.

DID YOU KNOW

As a naval centre, Halifax was especially busy during the war, with convoys of ships leaving regularly for Europe.

BOOM TIMES

In 1947, a huge oil field was found under the prairie at Leduc, Alberta. This was the beginning of an oil boom that made Alberta rich. In other parts of Canada, the mining and forestry industries boomed. British Columbia began an era of prosperity in 1952 when W.A.C. Bennett became premier with a program to build roads, railways and hydroelectric dams.

All these projects provided jobs for Canadians as well as for the thousands of immigrants who arrived after the war. Some chose to work in the major cities such as Montreal, Toronto and Winnipeg, where new suburbs were being built. (People didn't need to live near their work now that they could afford cars.) From 1952 on, Canadians had something else new — television.

The W.A.C. Bennett Dam provided a vast amount of electricity for B.C.

DID YOU KNOW

In 1950, the Red River flooded, covering one-sixth of Winnipeg and causing 100 000 people to leave their homes. Afterwards, a floodway (wide channel) was built to carry floodwater around Winnipeg.

Aboriginal People

The effects of the postwar boom were felt as far away as the Arctic, where companies were searching for minerals. Increasing contact with southerners had spread diseases among the Inuit. Many had caught tuberculosis (a disease that usually affects the lungs) and were being treated in southern hospitals. This meant they were totally out of contact with their families, sometimes for years.

The government wanted the Inuit to give up their hunting lifestyle and settle in permanent communities, where they could have medical clinics and schools. Some Inuit children were in residential schools — just like First Nations children.

First Nations people were no longer banned from holding traditional ceremonies, but they still had very few rights. They couldn't stop companies from digging for minerals on their reserves and were seldom given any of the profits.

DID YOU KNOW

In 1951, as a result of the efforts of Aboriginal groups, the Indian Act was revised to allow the potlatch and other ceremonies.

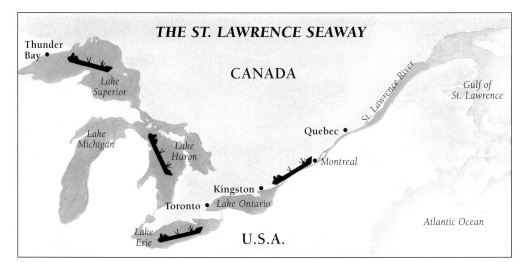

The St. Lawrence Seaway, a massive engineering project, was opened in 1959. Its canals and locks made it possible for large ships to sail far inland. The Seaway was built jointly by Canada and the United States.

On the World Scene

Overseas, Canada gained great prestige during this period. Canadian troops served in the Korean War (1950–53) to prevent communist North Korea from taking over South Korea. In 1956, Canada played a central role in resolving the Suez Crisis — a conflict in Egypt that threatened to spread into a major war. The Canadian politician Lester Pearson suggested that a United Nations Emergency Force be formed to act as the world's peacekeepers. The force kept the warring sides apart, and in 1957 Pearson was awarded the Nobel Peace Prize.

John Diefenbaker

"Dief the Chief"

In the federal election of 1957, the Liberal government of Louis St. Laurent was narrowly defeated by the Conservatives under John Diefenbaker. Hoping to get more seats in Parliament, Diefenbaker held another election the next year. This time he was stunningly successful, winning a record majority of 208 of 265 seats.

A lawyer from Saskatchewan, Diefenbaker was a passionate champion of the disadvantaged — people without power. His government gave all Canadians equal rights before the law. It also gave all Canadians, including Aboriginal people, the right to vote in federal elections.

James Gladstone

Ellen Fairclough

Georges Vanier

Diefenbaker was the first prime minister to appoint an Aboriginal person (James Gladstone) to the Senate and the first to appoint a woman (Ellen Fairclough) to the federal cabinet. He also arranged for the appointment of Canada's first French-Canadian governor general — war hero Georges Vanier.

Marilyn Bell swam 51.5 km (32 mi.) to cross Lake Ontario.

The Arts

Canadian culture blossomed during these years. The National Ballet was formed in 1951, the Stratford Festival opened in 1953 and in 1957 the Comédie-Canadienne was formed by the actor and playwright Gratien Gélinas.

Meanwhile, the National Film Board, formed just before the war, began to make dramas as well as its usual documentary films. Literature, painting and music also flourished. All the arts were given a boost in 1957 when the Canada Council was formed, with a large amount of money to support cultural projects.

Quick Facts
Sports Heroes

• *1947–48 Figure skater Barbara Ann Scott was the first North American skater to win both the World Championships (in 1947 and 1948) and an Olympic Games gold medal (in 1948).*

• *1950 Lionel Conacher was chosen Canada's all-round athlete of the half-century. The woman all-round athlete was Bobbie Rosenfeld.*

• *1954 Marilyn Bell (above), age 16, was the first person to swim across Lake Ontario.*

Prime Ministers' Timeline

Louis St. Laurent, 1948–57 (Liberal)   *John Diefenbaker, 1957–63 (Conservative)*

THE SWINGING SIXTIES

The 1960s was the decade of hippies and "flower power," when young people at folk festivals sang of peace and an end to injustice. In fact, Canada had already taken several steps toward becoming a just society that helped the needy.

Since the early 1940s, unemployment insurance had provided payments to Canadians who had no jobs. Since 1945, all families with children had received family allowance payments. From 1951 on, everyone over 70 received an old-age pension. Another type of pension, the Canada Pension Plan, came into action in 1966. It was brought in by the Liberal government of Lester Pearson.

The World's Fair, Expo '67, was held in Montreal.

Liberals in Power

The Liberals won the 1963 election largely because Diefenbaker was no longer popular. Among other things, he had put 14 000 people out of work by cancelling production of the Avro Arrow, a supersonic fighter plane.

Although the Liberals won the election, they held only a few more seats than the Conservatives. To stay in power, they needed the support of other parties. This gave the New Democratic Party (NDP) the chance to get the Liberals to carry out some NDP policies. One of these was medicare, which enabled poor as well as rich people to get the medical treatment they needed. An Act to set up nationwide medicare was passed in 1966.

PROFILE

TOMMY DOUGLAS

Thomas (Tommy) Douglas is called the Father of Medicare because when he was premier of Saskatchewan (1944–61) he arranged for the province to have a system of medicare — the first in Canada. Saskatchewan's doctors disliked the plan and tried to stop it, so medicare didn't come into effect in Saskatchewan until 1962. By then, Douglas had left to become national NDP leader.

Singer Buffy Sainte-Marie, born on the Piapot Reserve, Saskatchewan, became famous for such protest songs as "The Universal Soldier" and "Now That the Buffalo's Gone."

The Quiet Revolution

Dramatic events took place in Quebec during this period. For years, the province had been run by the dictatorlike government of Maurice Duplessis. In some ways, little had changed during the past century. The Catholic Church still controlled education, and English Canadians still controlled business.

When Jean Lesage became premier in 1960, his Liberal government set out to make Quebec more up-to-date — and more Quebec-owned. For example, they took over many privately owned electric-power companies. They also put education firmly under government control and reorganized it, providing more higher education, especially in the sciences. Other reforms were aimed to give Quebec a more important place in both Canada and the world.

"WE MUST BE 'MASTERS IN OUR OWN HOUSE.'"

Premier Jean Lesage

Quebec Nationalism

Lesage's reforms produced a surge of nationalism in Quebec — a pride in being Québécois. Poets, novelists, filmmakers and others celebrated Quebec's culture and history in their works. For instance, when Gilles Vigneault wrote the poem "Mon Pays" ("My Country"), he meant Quebec, not Canada.

More and more Québécois thought of their province as a distinct country, and some wanted it to become a separate nation. Others wanted to remain part of Canada but to increase the use of French in Quebec. Many Québécois had to speak English at work, because most top jobs in business were held by English Canadians. All of this worried Prime Minister Pearson, so in 1963 he set up a royal commission to look into relations between French and English Canadians.

Canada Celebrates

In 1965, Canada got a new flag, much to the fury of Diefenbaker and other pro-British patriots. They objected because the maple leaf flag didn't include the Union Jack, as the old flag had done. But Pearson wanted a totally Canadian flag. There were now many Canadians who didn't have British roots — and more would soon

The Parti Québécois

The Parti Québécois was founded in 1968 by René Lévesque (left) and others. Its aim was to make Quebec a separate nation while still sharing Canada's money system and other things. This proposed arrangement was called "sovereignty association."

Lester Pearson

be arriving. The Pearson government's 1967 Immigration Act removed all restrictions based on race and nationality. In future, immigrants would be accepted according to their education and skills.

July 1, 1967, was Canada's hundredth birthday, and Canadians celebrated all year with parties, competitions and exhibitions. The greatest was Expo '67, the World's Fair held in Montreal. As Canadians welcomed visitors from all over the world, they felt immensely proud of all that their country had achieved in the past century.

Prime Ministers' Timeline

Lester Pearson, 1963–68 (Liberal)

THE TRUDEAU YEARS

Pierre Trudeau became prime minister in 1968 on a wave of enthusiasm. The son of a French-Canadian father and an English-Canadian mother, Trudeau was from both major cultural groups. As well as being impressively intelligent, he had a free and easy style that fitted the times. Young people flocked to see him.

Trudeau had definite ideas about what he wanted to do for Canada, and he went ahead and acted on them even though some people objected. During his 15 years in office, he changed Canada in many important ways.

The October Crisis of 1970

A few Quebec separatists were extremists who used violence. In October 1970, a group called the FLQ kidnapped two prominent men and killed one of them. They hoped to force the government to let Quebec separate. But Trudeau stood firm. The crisis ended when the FLQ released their surviving hostage in exchange for a flight to Cuba.

Daring to Be Different

In 1969, the Trudeau government passed the Official Languages Act. The Act said that both French and English must be available to people throughout Canada in the courts and all other branches of the federal government. Most French Canadians working in federal jobs were already bilingual, but most English Canadians were not, and many didn't want to learn French.

Then, during the October Crisis, Trudeau upset more Canadians by using the War Measures Act, which allowed people to be jailed without trial. More than 450 Québécois were jailed during the crisis. Most of them had done nothing illegal and didn't approve of violence, but they were known to be separatists.

DID YOU KNOW

New Brunswick made English and French official languages in 1969. In all other provinces, except Quebec, English is the official language.

Troops were called in to help the police during the crisis.

Robert Bourassa

More Changes in Quebec

Robert Bourassa, the new Liberal premier of Quebec, was against the separatists but was a strong supporter of Quebec's French culture. To prevent the language from dying out, he made French the only official language in Quebec and made most immigrant children go to French-speaking schools. These measures didn't go far enough for many Québécois, and in 1976 they elected a separatist government — the Parti Québécois (PQ) — led by René Lévesque.

The PQ's victory sent shock waves throughout the country. What would happen to Canada if Quebec left? And what would happen to English Canadians living in Quebec? When the PQ passed laws increasing the use of French, many English Canadians left the province. Several large companies moved their head offices to Ontario.

Before the PQ could take Quebec out of Canada, it had to hold a referendum — a province-wide vote — to be sure people wanted separation. When the referendum was held in 1980, the majority voted against it. Lévesque was very disappointed, but he vowed to try again. "*À la prochaine*" ("Until next time") he told his supporters.

The "yes" and "no" sides both had strong supporters in the Quebec referendum.

First Nations on the Move

During the 1970s, Aboriginal people were actively trying to get more control over their lives. They were furious about a 1969 "white paper" — a government report on policy. It proposed that the federal government assimilate Aboriginal people, making them like other Canadians, and it ignored the importance of treaty rights and land claims.

In reaction, the First Nations increased their efforts to claim their rights. In 1975, the Cree and Inuit of northern Quebec won an important land claims battle — they made the province pay them for the land it needed for a huge hydroelectric project. By the James Bay Agreement, the Cree and Inuit received $225 million from the province. As well, they could carry on hunting and fishing in the area and run many of their own affairs, including their schools.

In 1980, chiefs from across Canada formed the Assembly of First Nations to press for other changes.

In the Canada–Soviet Hockey Series of 1972, Paul Henderson scored the most famous goal in hockey history, with just 34 seconds remaining in the game.

DID YOU KNOW

In the 1970s, Canada "went metric," converting imperial measurements such as "feet" and "pints" into "metres" and "litres."

Science and Technology

Canada's first satellite, *Alouette I*, was taken into space aboard a U.S. rocket in 1962. In the 1970s, Canada's first communications satellites were launched. They provided better telephone and television service and made it more widely available.

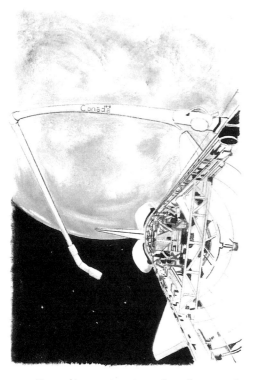

Canadian scientists also designed the Canadarm — a mechanical arm to handle satellites and other objects floating in space. It was first used aboard the space shuttle *Columbia*. Another scientific landmark occurred in 1971, when Canada's Gerhard Herzberg won the Nobel Prize for Chemistry.

A Changing Society

Every advance in science and technology had a direct effect on Canadians' lives. In Labrador, for instance, the huge hydroelectric project on the Churchill River (1966–74) gave jobs to many Newfoundlanders. In 1979, the discovery of the Hibernia oil field off the Newfoundland coast offered another source of work. But tragedy struck in 1982, when the drilling rig *Ocean Ranger* capsized and sank in a storm, drowning its 84 crew members.

The new technology affected women across Canada. During the past 30 years, the invention of dishwashers and other labour-saving machines had made it easier for women to go out to work. They didn't need to spend all day doing housework. In some families, men helped with the household chores. Changing times had brought changing attitudes.

Women were also beginning to hold top positions — in 1974, Bette Stephenson became president of the Canadian Medical Association, and in 1980 Lois Wilson became moderator of the United Church of Canada.

Jeanne Sauvé

Bertha Wilson was appointed in 1982 to the Supreme Court of Canada, and in 1984 Jeanne Sauvé was appointed governor general, after being speaker of the House of Commons.

All these appointments were "firsts" for women. They were partly the result of the Women's Movement, which had been trying to get women accepted as equals of men in all areas, including pay.

Multiculturalism

In this changing society, Canadians were more tolerant to people different from themselves. In 1971, Trudeau announced a policy of multiculturalism, which encouraged all ethnic groups to share their culture with others. Many were already doing so, simply by opening ethnic restaurants or stores. Since the change in the immigration laws (page 61), people had come to Canada from all parts of the world. The newcomers included some 20 000 South Asian refugees who had been living in East Africa but were no longer welcome there. Canada also welcomed about 75 000 "boat people" — refugees from Vietnam, Laos and Cambodia who fled from their homes in crowded ships. This crisis was at its height during the brief government of Joe Clark, who helped the boat people immigrate.

Terry Fox won the hearts of Canadians for his courage in 1980, when he set off to run across the country to raise funds for cancer research. Each year, thousands of Canadians raise more money by taking part in the Terry Fox Marathon of Hope.

Canadian Astronauts

In 1984, Marc Garneau was the first Canadian to go into space. The first Canadian woman in space was Roberta Bondar in 1992.

The New Constitution

When Trudeau again became prime minister, he was determined to "bring the constitution home." The constitution was the British North America Act, which had founded Canada in 1867. Because it was a British Act, any changes to it that Canada wanted had to be made by the British parliament. In the past, Canadian politicians had often tried to write a Canadian Act. But they could never agree on the rules governing how changes would be made to the Act.

For more than a year, Trudeau negotiated with the premiers of the provinces, trying to get them to agree on the details of the new Act. Eventually, all provinces except Quebec agreed, and the Constitution Act was signed by Queen Elizabeth during her visit to Canada in 1982 (above). The Act includes the Canadian Charter of Rights and Freedoms, which says that all people are equal before the law, whatever their race, sex or religion. It guarantees Aboriginal rights and supports "the multicultural heritage of Canadians."

Prime Ministers' Timeline

Pierre Elliott Trudeau, 1968–79 (Liberal)

Joseph Clark, 1979–80 (Conservative)

Trudeau, 1980–84 (Liberal)

THE WAY FORWARD

Since the 1980s, Canada has become a much more multicultural society. School concerts now include songs of many religions, instead of celebrating only Christian festivals. But although Canada's people come from all over the world, its two major cultural groups are still French and English.

Quebec, especially, sees itself as one of *two* — French and English. But many Canadians see Quebec as one of *ten* provinces. This was partly why Quebec didn't agree to the 1982 Constitution Act. The Act didn't give Quebec the power it wanted to protect its culture. When Brian Mulroney became prime minister, he tried to change the constitution in a way that Quebec would approve.

All provinces have welcomed immigrants from many parts of the world. Canada's multicultural mix can be seen in some of the people chosen for leading positions. Left to right: Lincoln Alexander, son of West Indian immigrants, lieutenant-governor of Ontario, 1985–91; Joseph Ghiz, of Lebanese origin, premier of Prince Edward Island, 1986–93; Adrienne Clarkson, born Hong Kong, governor general, 1999–2005; Ujjal Dosanjh, a Sikh, premier of British Columbia, 2000–01

The Search for Unity

In 1987, Mulroney met with the premiers of the ten provinces at Meech Lake, near Ottawa. After much discussion, they signed an accord that declared Quebec a "distinct society" and gave it and other provinces some new powers. But many Canadians disliked the accord. Some thought it gave the provinces too much power. Others said it favoured Quebec. When the accord was put before the provincial legislatures, it didn't get approval in Manitoba and Newfoundland.

Mulroney tried again with the Charlottetown Accord in 1992. This time he met with Aboriginal leaders and the leaders of the two territories as well as the premiers. But most Canadians, including most Québécois, voted against it.

The Conservatives under Brian Mulroney set a new record in the 1984 election, winning 211 seats. In the 1993 election, they won only two seats.

DID YOU KNOW

Elijah Harper, an Aboriginal member of the Manitoba legislature, blocked the Meech Lake Accord by refusing to agree to it. The terms of the accord made it unlikely that the Yukon and the Northwest Territories (where many Aboriginal people live) would ever be able to become provinces.

A Divided Canada

Many Canadians also disliked Mulroney's Free Trade Agreement (FTA), which made trade easier between Canada and the United States. It went into effect in 1989 and helped big business. So did a later agreement that included Mexico. But opponents said that free trade gave Americans too much influence over Canada. They said Canada would become like the United States and lose its unique culture, along with other Canadian things such as medicare.

In the first few years of free trade, many Canadians lost their jobs. There was an economic depression, and big American companies shut down their factories in Canada rather than closing U.S. factories. Meanwhile, prices went up, partly because Mulroney had brought in the goods and services tax (GST).

The Liberals in Power

By 1993, Mulroney had become extremely unpopular, and he resigned. The Conservatives chose a woman, Kim Campbell, to succeed him. But the party was so hated that it was almost wiped out in the 1993 election, and the Liberals took over, led by Jean Chrétien.

Chrétien remained prime minister until 2003 and was succeeded by Paul Martin, also a Liberal. Then in 2006, the Conservatives won the election and their leader, Stephen Harper, became prime minister.

Quebec-born former prime minister Jean Chrétien believed in a strong, united Canada.

Nunavut

In 1999, the Inuit got something they had been striving for since the 1970s — the eastern portion of the Northwest Territories became a separate territory called Nunavut. The name means "our land" in the Inuktitut language. About 85 percent of Nunavut's people are Inuit.

Although Nunavut is not a province, it is run largely by Inuit, who hold senior positions in the public service as well as in government. Paul Okalik became the first premier.

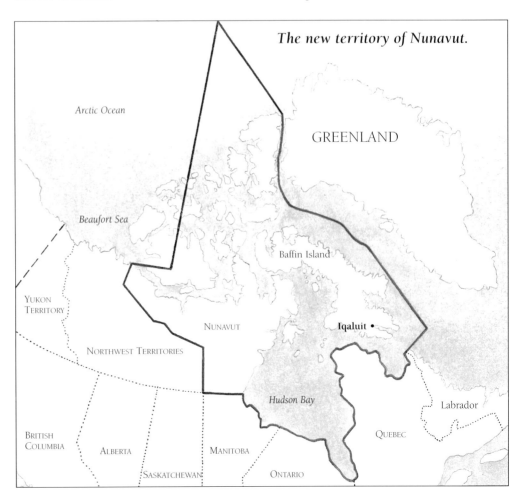

The new territory of Nunavut.

Another Quebec Referendum

Since the failure of the Charlottetown Accord, the separatists had grown stronger, winning the 1994 Quebec election. In a referendum the next year, they gained almost enough votes to allow Quebec to begin the process of separating from Canada. They were inspired by the fiery speeches of Lucien Bouchard, leader of the Bloc Québécois (a separatist party in the Parliament of Canada). He later became premier of Quebec (1996–2001).

Chief Joseph Gosnell was the leading negotiator of the Nisga'a treaty on behalf of his people.

Hockey player Wayne Gretzky was chosen Canadian male athlete of the twentieth century. Canada's female athlete of the century was skier Nancy Greene.

The Nisga'a Treaty

Another landmark in the late 1990s was the Nisga'a treaty, the result of land claims in British Columbia. The treaty made the Nisga'a people owners of some of their ancient lands in northwest B.C. It said they could elect their own government, which could make its own laws. The laws would affect all on Nisga'a territory but had to fit with other Canadian laws. The Nisga'a treaty serves as a model as other First Nations seek a settlement of long-standing land claims.

Canada and the World

Canada took part in the American-led Gulf War against Iraq in 1991 but not the Iraq War that began in 2003. Instead, Canadian forces went to Afghanistan to be peacekeepers in that war-torn land. Their job was to make the country safe for the Afghan people, though it has meant taking part in the fighting. Canadian forces have helped in many places, including New Orleans in 2005 after Hurricane Katrina hit the city.

Canada also continues to shine in sports and the arts, with such stars as Steve Nash and Avril Lavigne.

Canadian peacekeepers have helped people in more than 40 different countries across the world.

When the Red River flooded in 1997, it formed a huge inland sea that spread from the U.S. border to the suburbs of Winnipeg.

Important scientific awards have been won by Canadians, such as Nobel Prize winners John Polanyi (Chemistry, 1986), Michael Smith (Chemistry, 1993) and Bertram Brockhouse (Physics, 1994).

Canadian scientists have made a new, even better Canadarm. In 2006, astronaut Steve MacLean visited the International Space Station and became the first Canadian to operate Canadarm2.

And what about Canada's future? Whether or not Quebec remains part of Canada, the country will still be home to many Canadians of French origin. And it will still be a nation that was shaped by people of different languages and cultures who found a way of living together in peace.

The Environment

Canadians have always helped one another during natural disasters, such as the Manitoba flood of 1997 or the 1998 ice storm in Quebec and Ontario. But people tend not to notice long-term problems, which may be even more disastrous. The disappearance of cod off the east coast — the result of overfishing — has had a terrible effect on Atlantic Canada. In Newfoundland, a whole way of life disappeared, and people couldn't find work.

Other long-term problems range from sea ice shrinking in the Arctic to polluted air in the south. In 2008, the government announced a plan to reduce the causes of greenhouse gas in Canada by 20 percent by the year 2020. This is a step towards protecting both the environment and the health of Canadians. But there is still much more work to be done.

The New Age

Fortunately, Canada has a wealth of good scientists. This is the most scientific age Canadians have ever known, with computers in many homes as well as in the schools.

The Confederation Bridge, built in 1997, joins Prince Edward Island and New Brunswick. It is 12.9 km (8 mi.) long.

Prime Ministers' Timeline

John Turner, June–Sept. 1984 (Liberal)	Brian Mulroney, 1984–93 (Conservative)	Kim Campbell, June–Nov. 1993 (Conservative)	Jean Chrétien, 1993–2003 (Liberal)	Paul Martin, 2003–2006 (Liberal)	Stephen Harper, 2006– (Conservative)

TIMELINE

Thousands of years ago	Aboriginal people living in North America
c. 1000	Viking settlement on Newfoundland
1497	Cabot lands on Newfoundland
1534	Cartier explores Gulf of St. Lawrence
1535–36	Cartier visits Stadacona (Quebec)
1541–42	Cartier's third voyage
1576–78	Frobisher's three voyages to the Arctic
1583	Gilbert claims Newfoundland for England
1605	Port-Royal built by French
1608	Champlain founds Quebec
1610	Hudson explores Hudson Bay
1642	Montreal founded
1663	New France made a royal colony
1670	Hudson's Bay Company founded
1690	Kelsey is first European to see Canadian prairies
1713	Treaty of Utrecht
	Nova Scotia officially becomes a British colony
1731–43	The La Vérendryes explore west to the Saskatchewan River
1749	Cornwallis founds Halifax
1754	Henday reaches present-day Alberta
1755	Deportation of Acadians begins
1756	Outbreak of Seven Years' War
1759	Battle of Plains of Abraham
1763	Treaty of Paris ends Seven Years' War
	Royal Proclamation establishes Province of Quebec
1769	Colony of Prince Edward Island established
1774	Quebec Act
1775–83	American Revolution
1778	Cook lands on Vancouver Island
1784	Colony of New Brunswick formed
1791	Constitutional Act creates Upper and Lower Canada
1793	Alexander Mackenzie reaches Pacific Ocean overland
1812	Red River Settlement begun
	Outbreak of War of 1812
1814	Treaty of Ghent ends War of 1812
1830s–60s	Underground Railroad
1837–38	Rebellions in Lower and Upper Canada
1841	Upper and Lower Canada are joined to create Province of Canada
1846–48	Massive immigration of Irish fleeing the famine in Ireland
1848	Nova Scotia and Province of Canada get responsible government
1849	Vancouver Island made a British colony

1851	Prince Edward Island gets responsible government
1854	New Brunswick gets responsible government
	Reciprocity Treaty signed with United States
1855	Newfoundland gets responsible government
1857	First oil well in North America dug near Petrolia, Canada West
1858	Fraser River gold rush begins
	Mainland British Columbia made into a colony
1866	Vancouver Island and mainland British Columbia become one colony called British Columbia
1867	Dominion of Canada formed with four provinces: New Brunswick, Nova Scotia, Ontario and Quebec
1869–70	Louis Riel leads Red River Rising
1870	Hudson's Bay Company sells its territory to Canada
	Manitoba becomes Canada's fifth province
1871	British Columbia becomes Canada's sixth province
1873	Prince Edward Island becomes Canada's seventh province
1874	North-West Mounted Police (est. 1873) arrive in western prairies
1874–77	"Indian Treaties" give Canadian government most of the prairie people's lands
1885	Northwest Rebellion
	Canadian Pacific Railway completed
1897	Large-scale settlement of the West begins
1897–99	Klondike gold rush
1898	Yukon Territory created
1899–1902	South African (Boer) War
1905	Alberta and Saskatchewan become provinces
1914	World War I begins
1916	Manitoba is first province to give women the vote
1917	Battle of Vimy Ridge
	Halifax explosion
1918	World War I ends
	Women get the vote in federal elections
	League of Indians of Canada formed
1919	Winnipeg General Strike
1920	Group of Seven hold first show
1921	Banting and Best discover how to make insulin
1929	Great Depression begins
	Persons Case won

1931	Statute of Westminster
1934	Commission of Government starts in Newfoundland
1936	Canadian Broadcasting Corporation formed
1939	National Film Board created
	World War II begins
	Great Depression ends
1944	D-Day
1945	World War II ends
1947	Leduc oil find starts oil boom in Alberta
1949	Newfoundland joins Canada
1950	Korean War begins
	Winnipeg Flood
1952	W.A.C. Bennett becomes premier of British Columbia
1953	Korean War ends
1957	Canada Council formed
1959	St. Lawrence Seaway opened
1960	Quebec's Quiet Revolution begins
1961	New Democratic Party formed
1962	*Alouette I*, Canada's first satellite, launched
1965	Canada gets maple leaf flag
1966	Canada Pension Plan begins
	Medical Care Act (medicare) passed
1967	Canada celebrates its one-hundredth birthday
1968	Parti Québécois formed
1969	Official Languages Act
	New Brunswick makes English and French official languages
	White paper on Aboriginal people
1970	October Crisis
1971	Trudeau announces policy of multiculturalism
1975	James Bay Agreement
1976	Parti Québécois elected in Quebec
1980	First referendum about Quebec separation
1982	Constitution Act and Charter of Rights and Freedoms
1987	Meech Lake Accord
	Reform Party formed
1989	Free Trade Agreement goes into effect
1991	Bloc Québécois formed
1992	Charlottetown Accord
1995	Second referendum on Quebec separation
1997	Confederation Bridge joins Prince Edward Island to mainland
	Manitoba Flood
1999	Nunavut formed
2000	Canadian Alliance formed
	Nisga'a Treaty (agreed 1998) becomes law
2001	New Canadarm (*Canadarm2*) attached to International Space Station
2003	Progressive Conservative Party and Canadian Alliance merge to become the Conservative Party of Canada
	Canadian peacekeepers sent to Afghanistan

INDEX